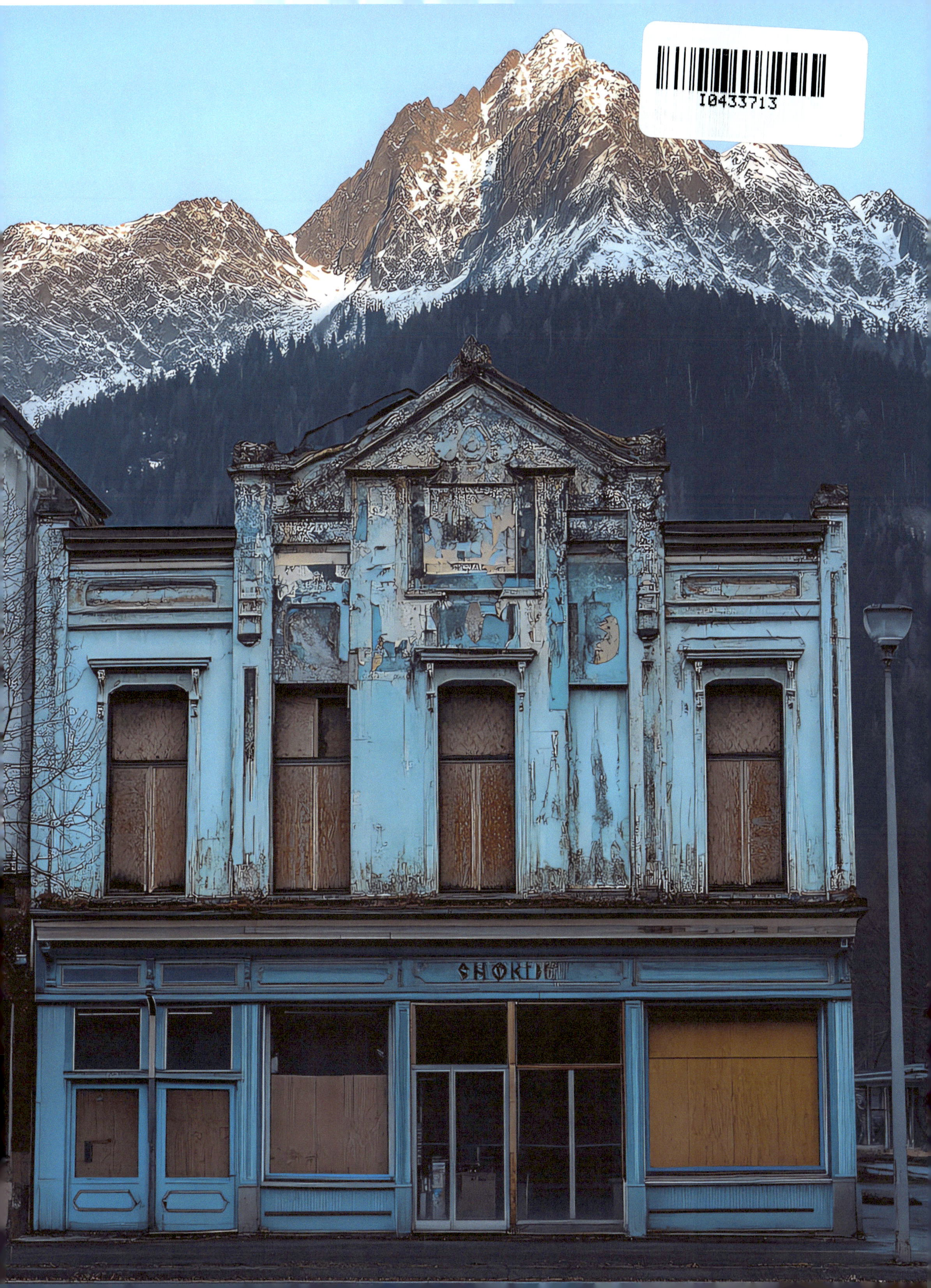

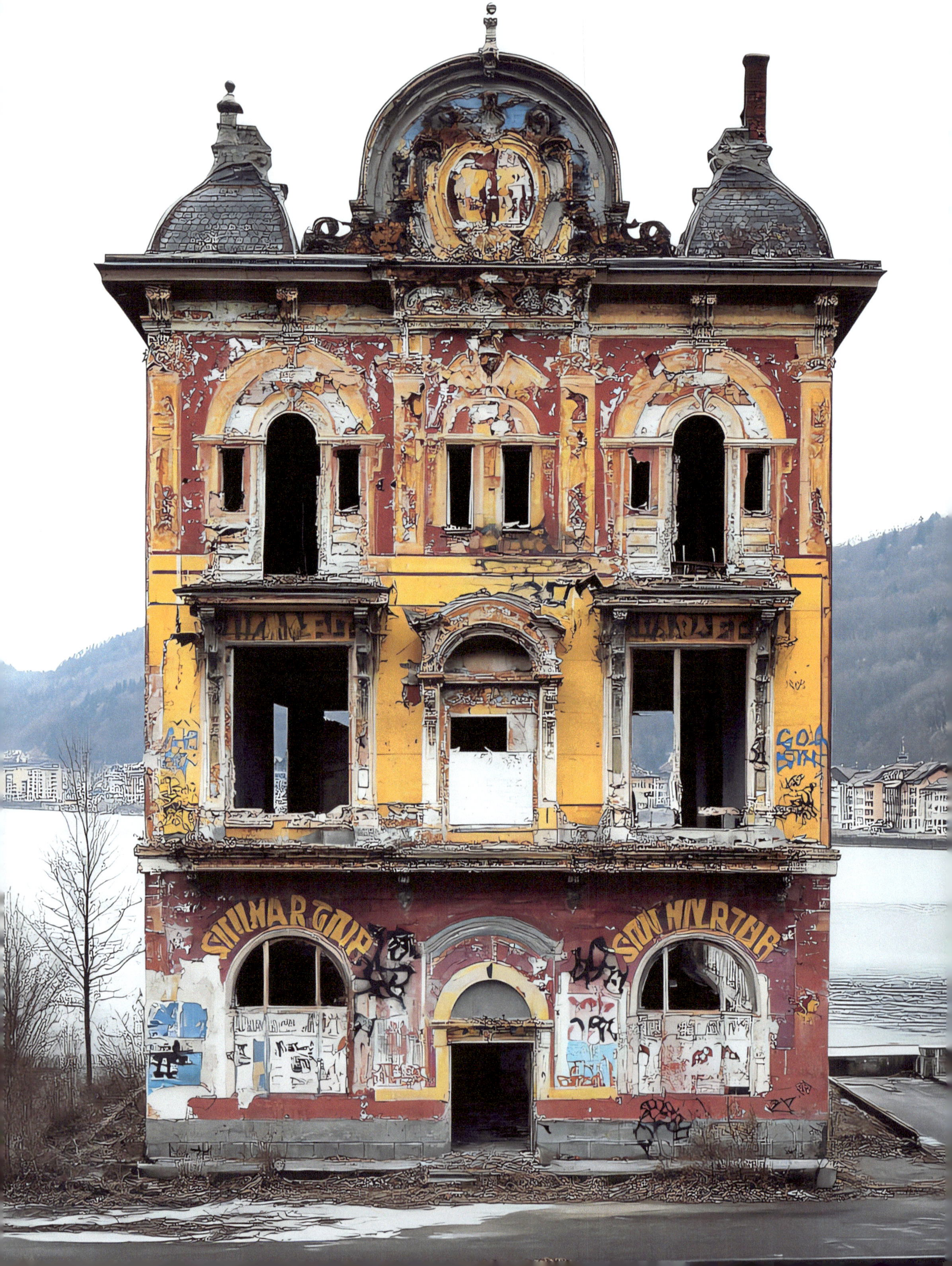

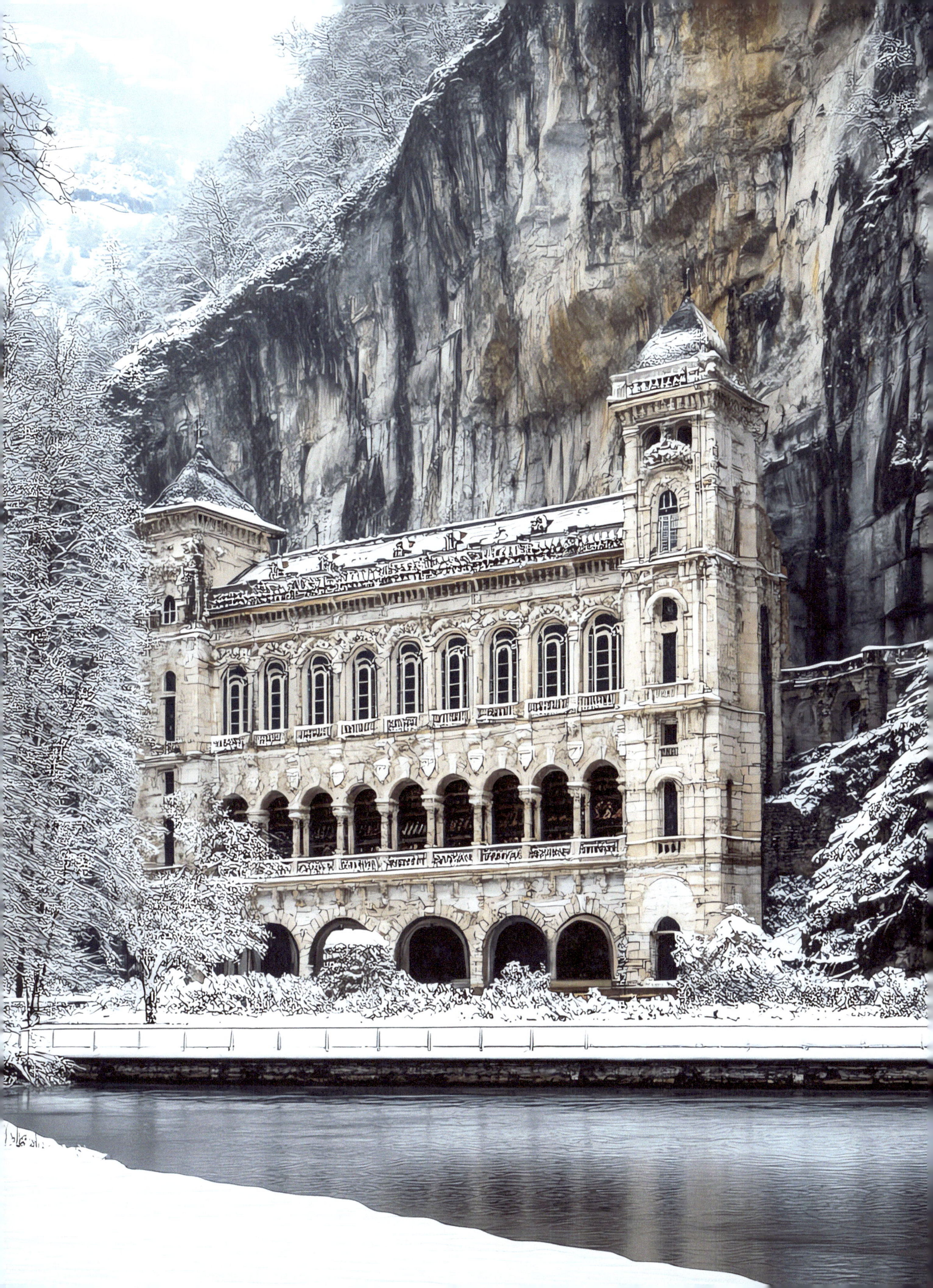

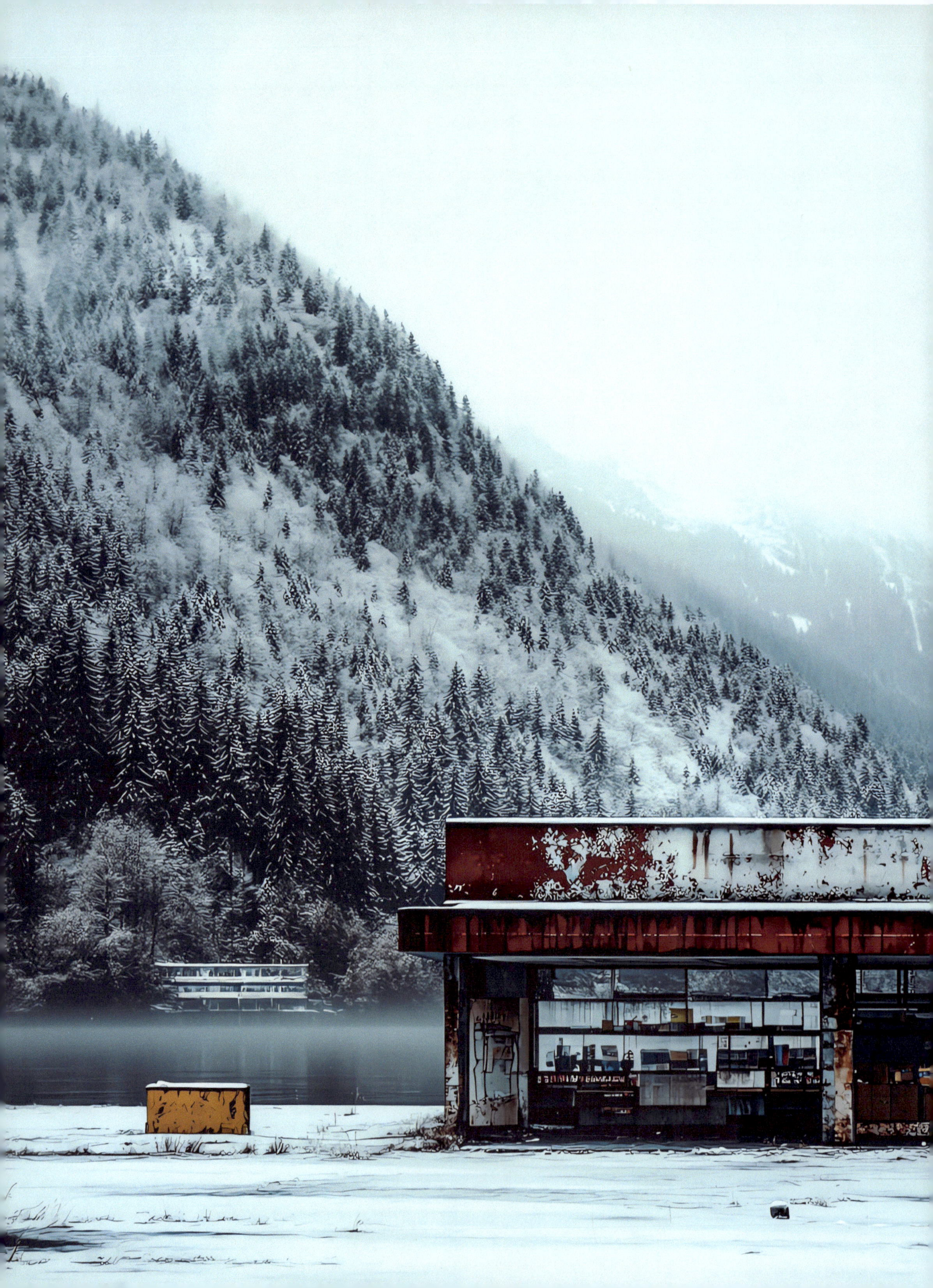

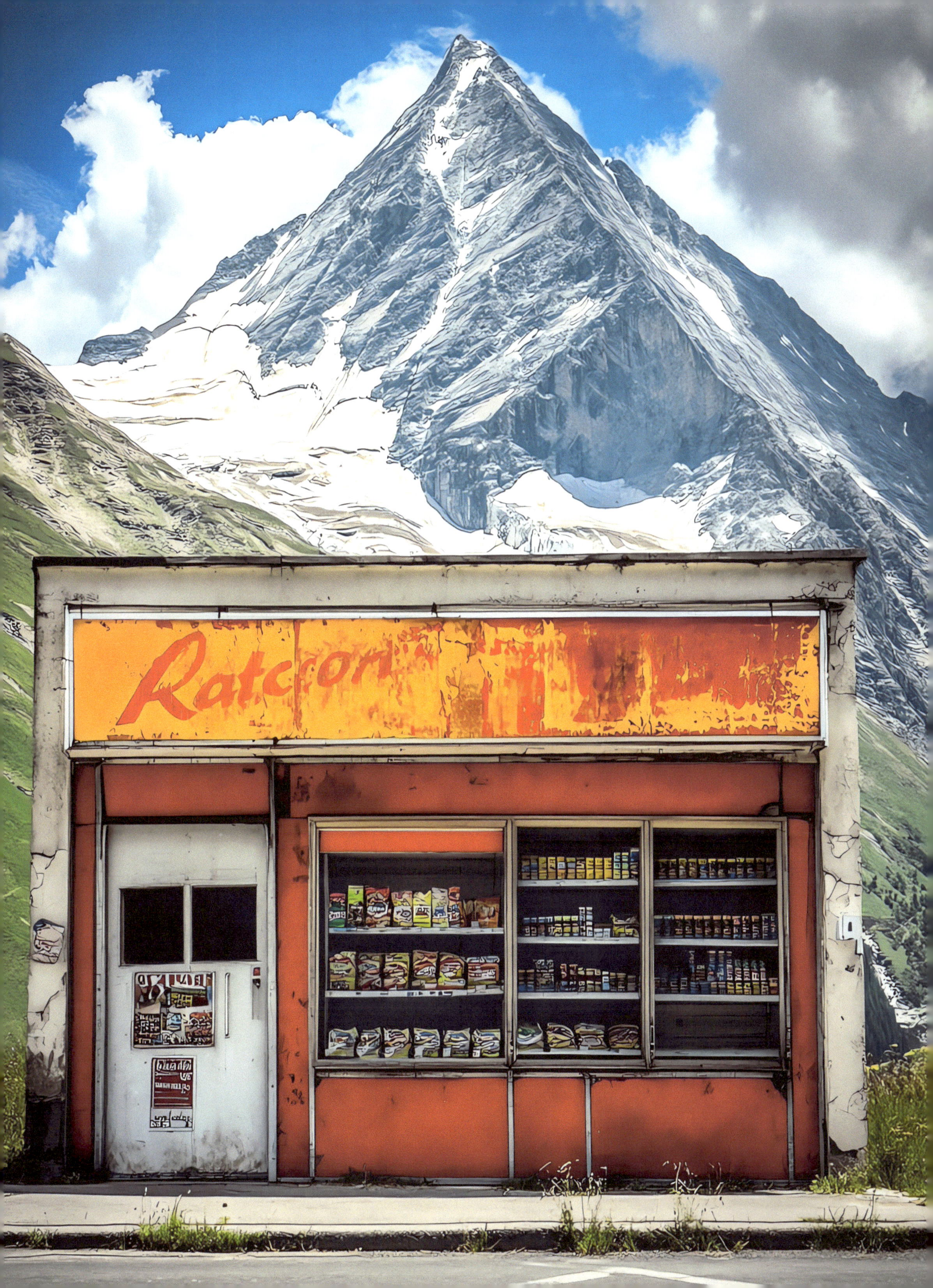

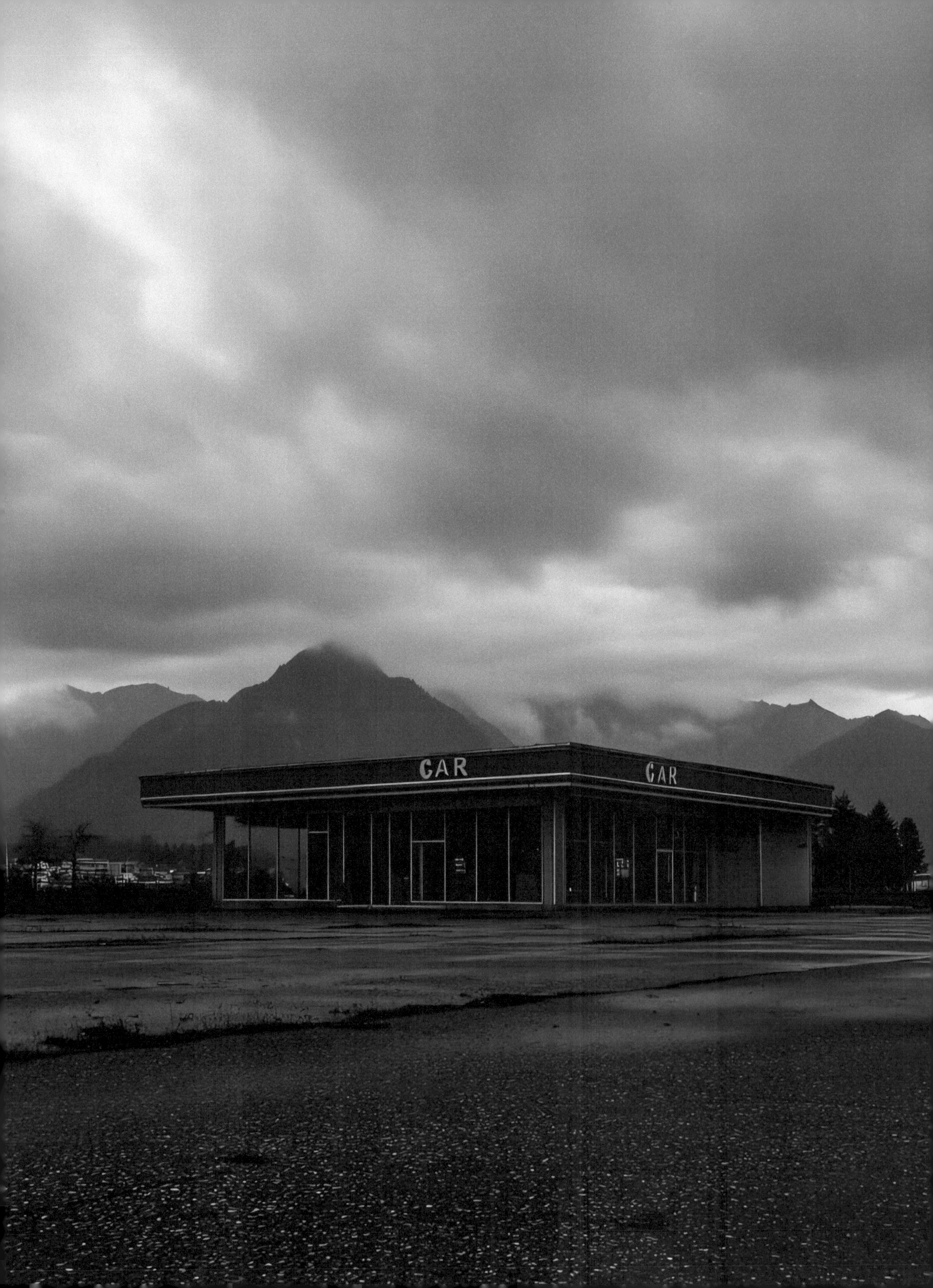
CAR
CAR

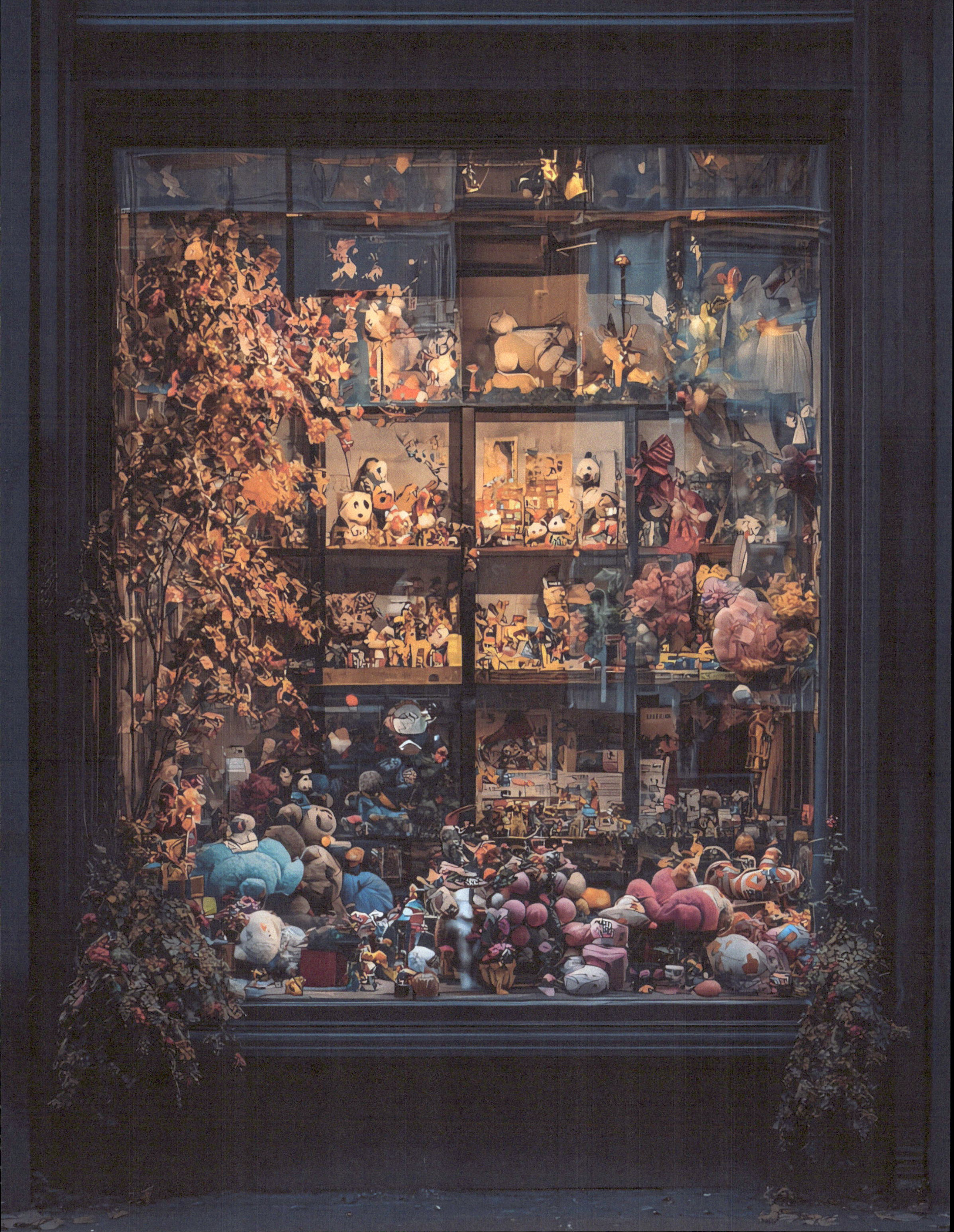

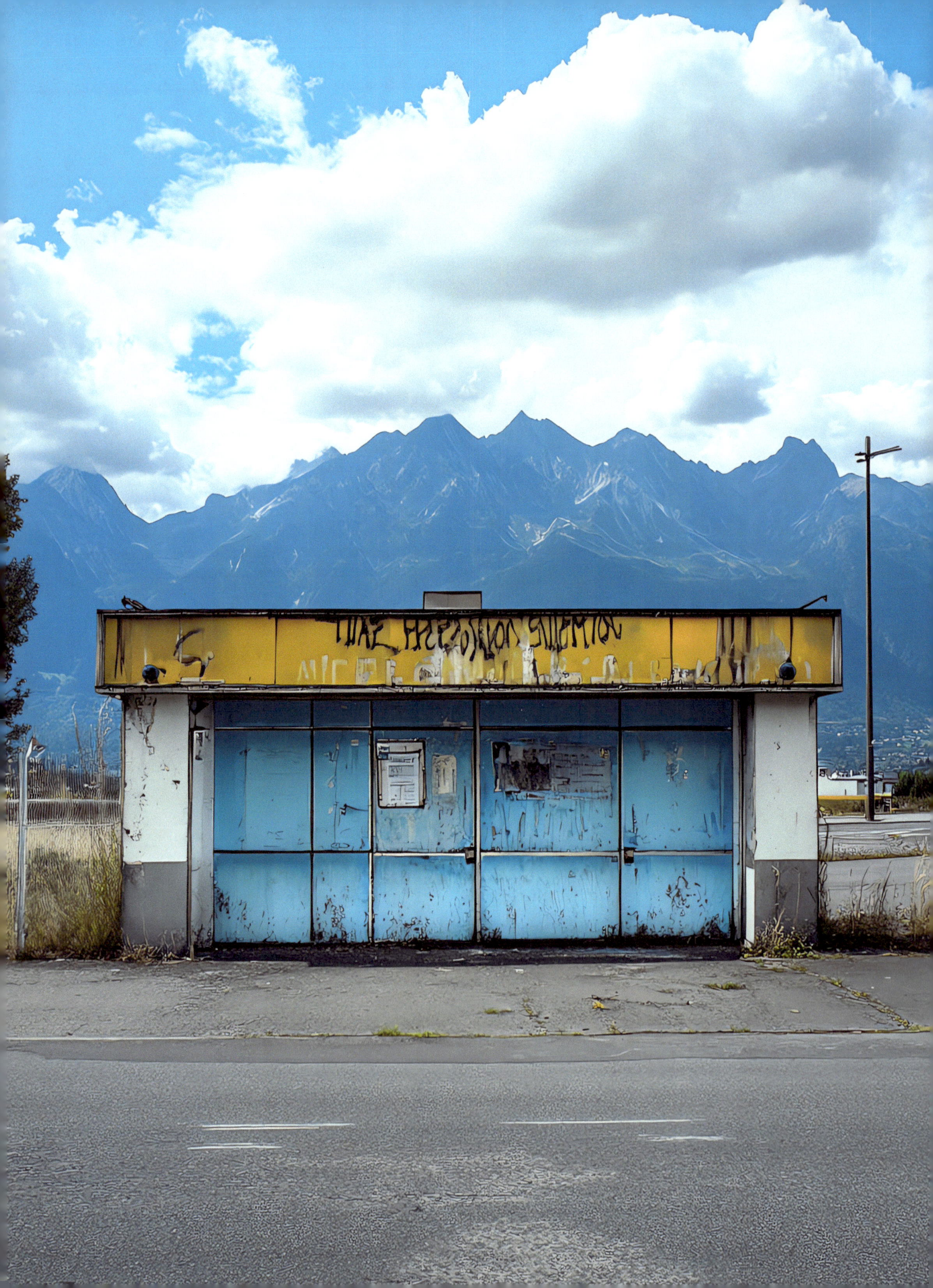

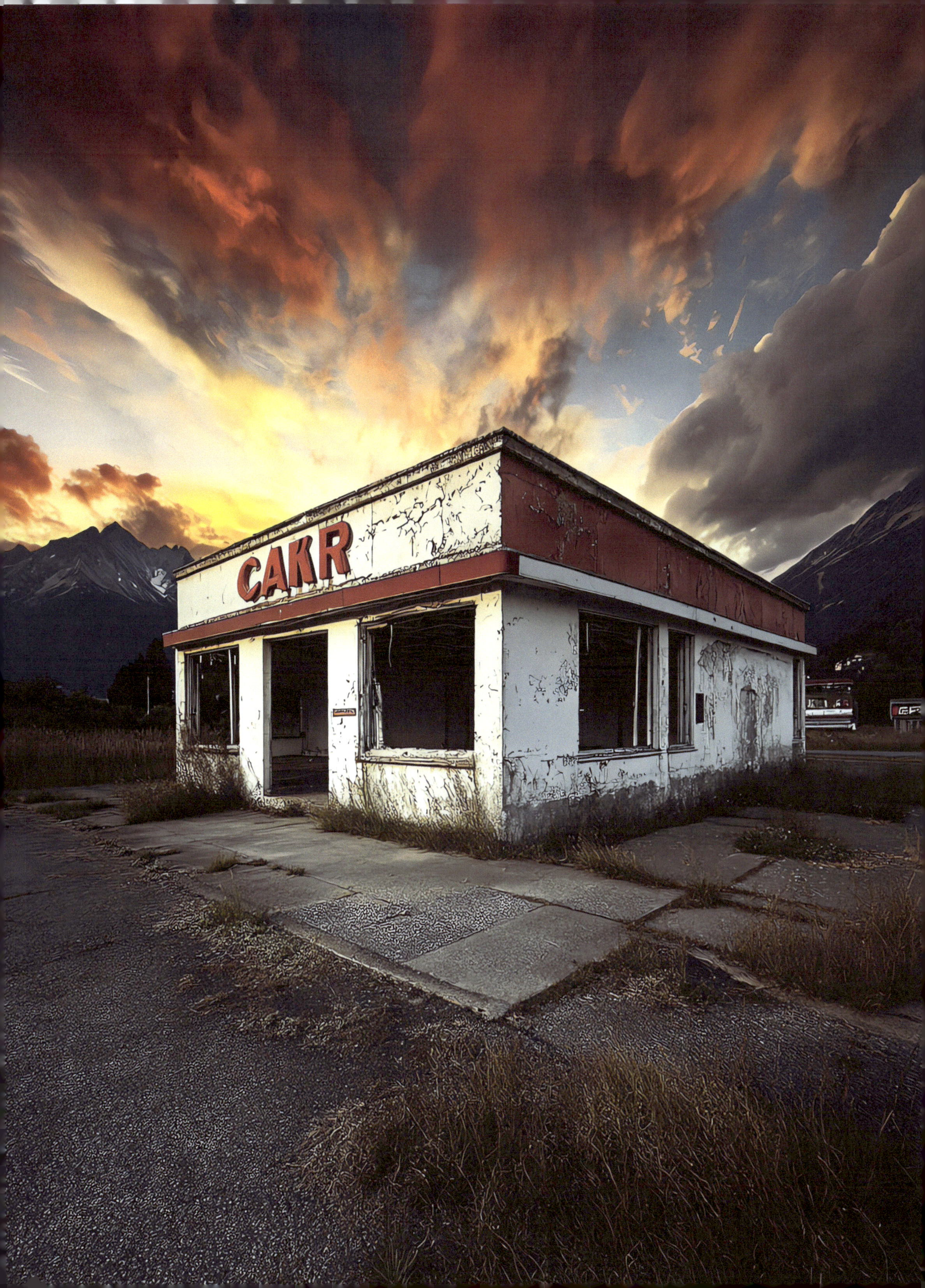
CAKR

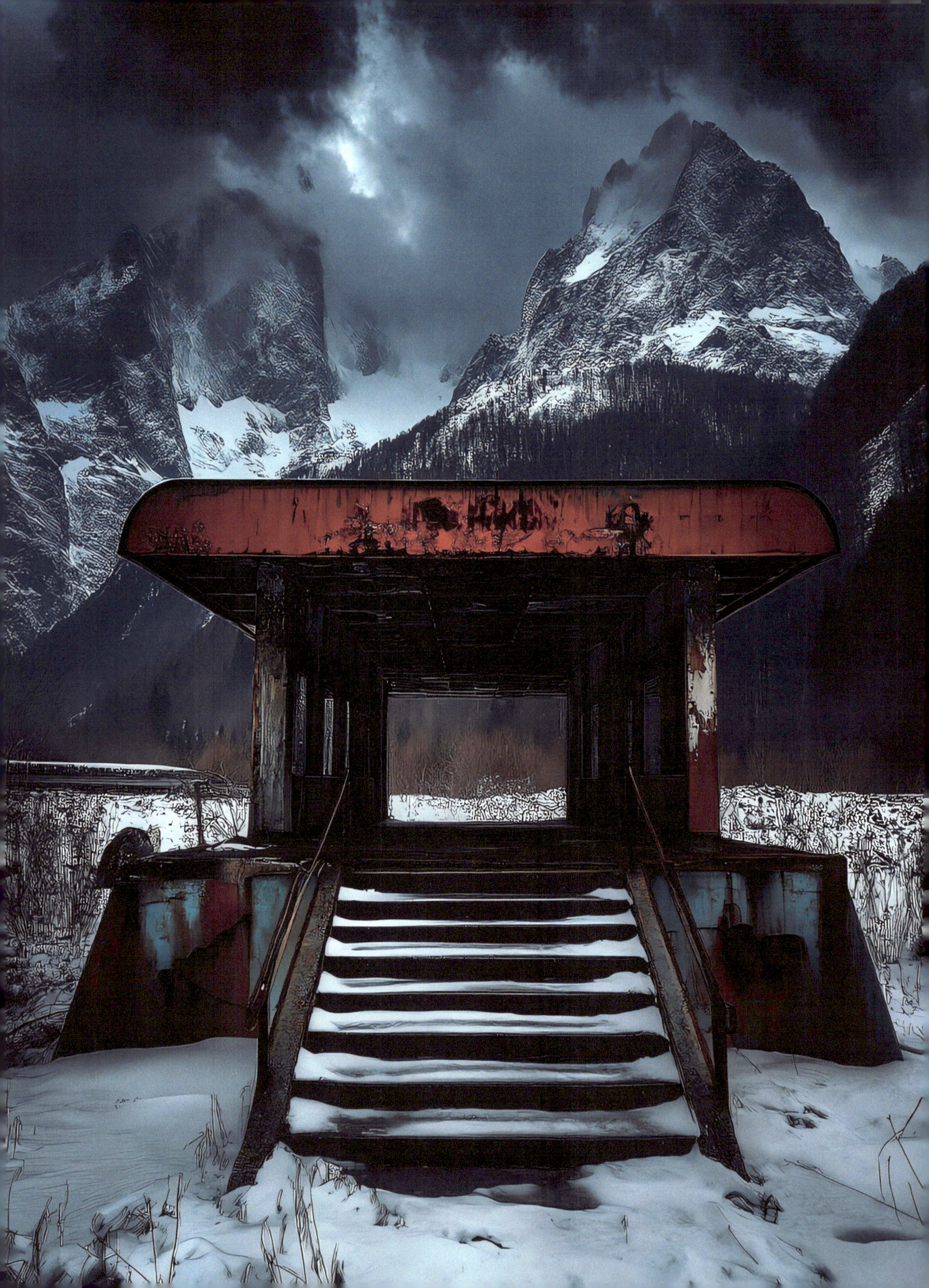

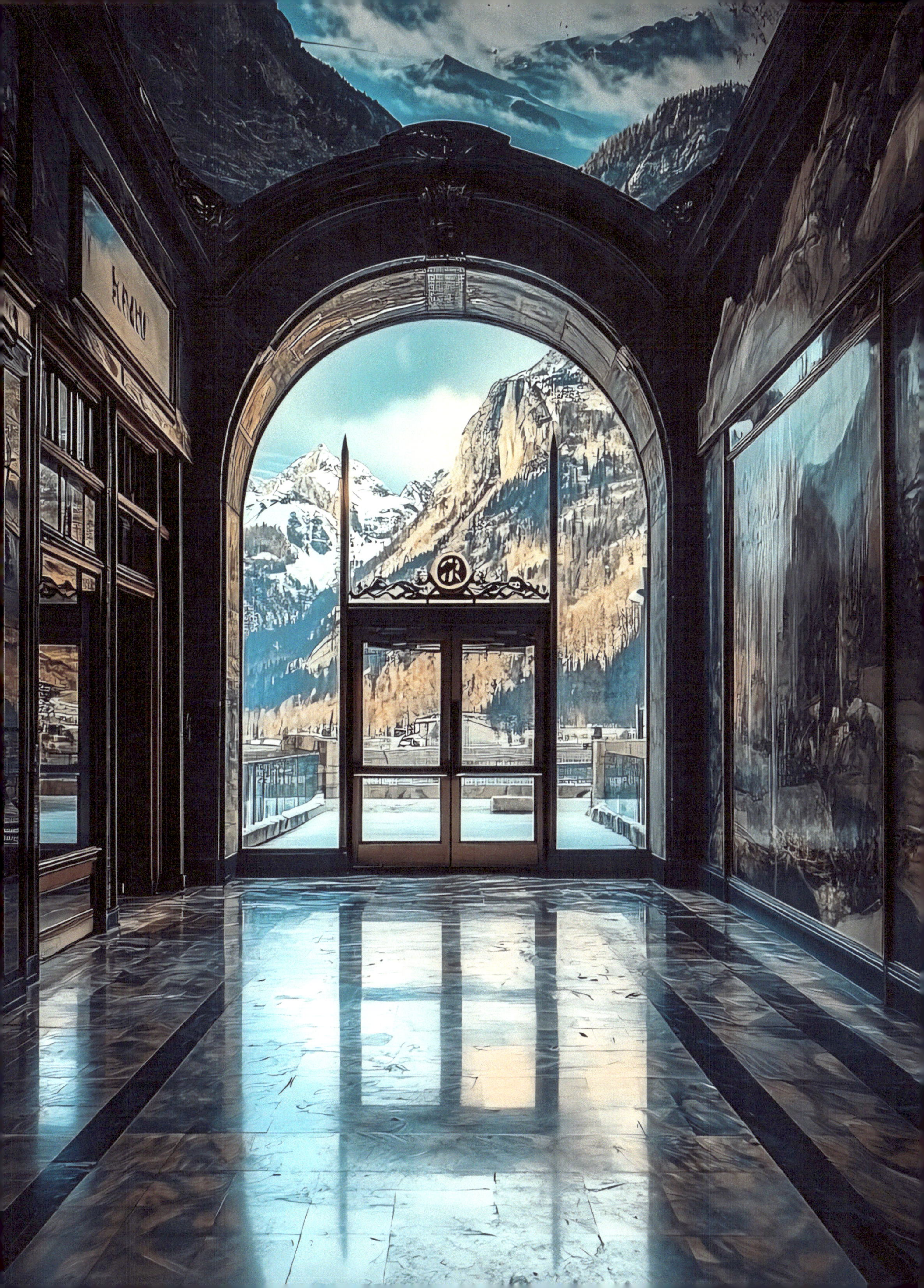

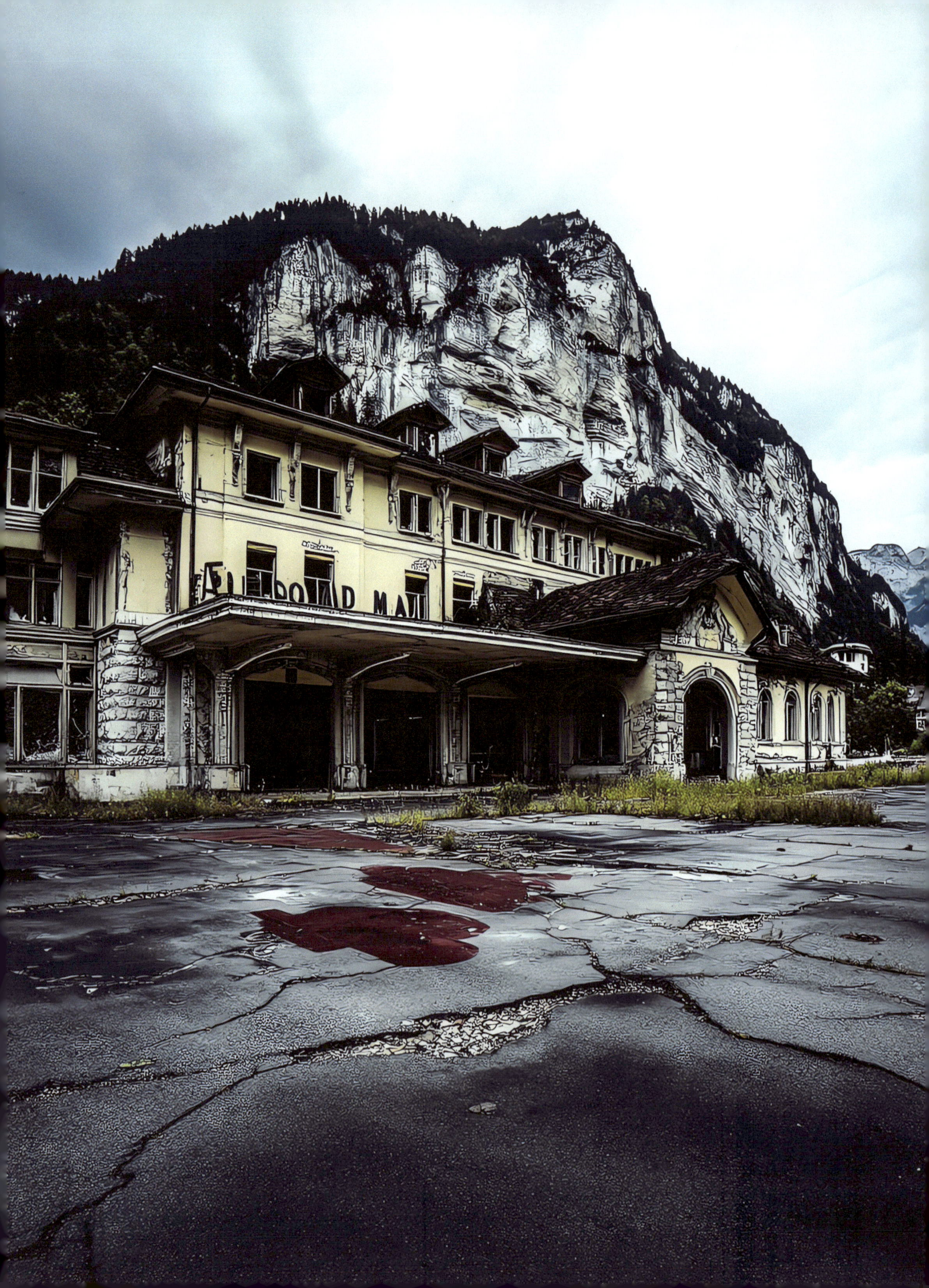

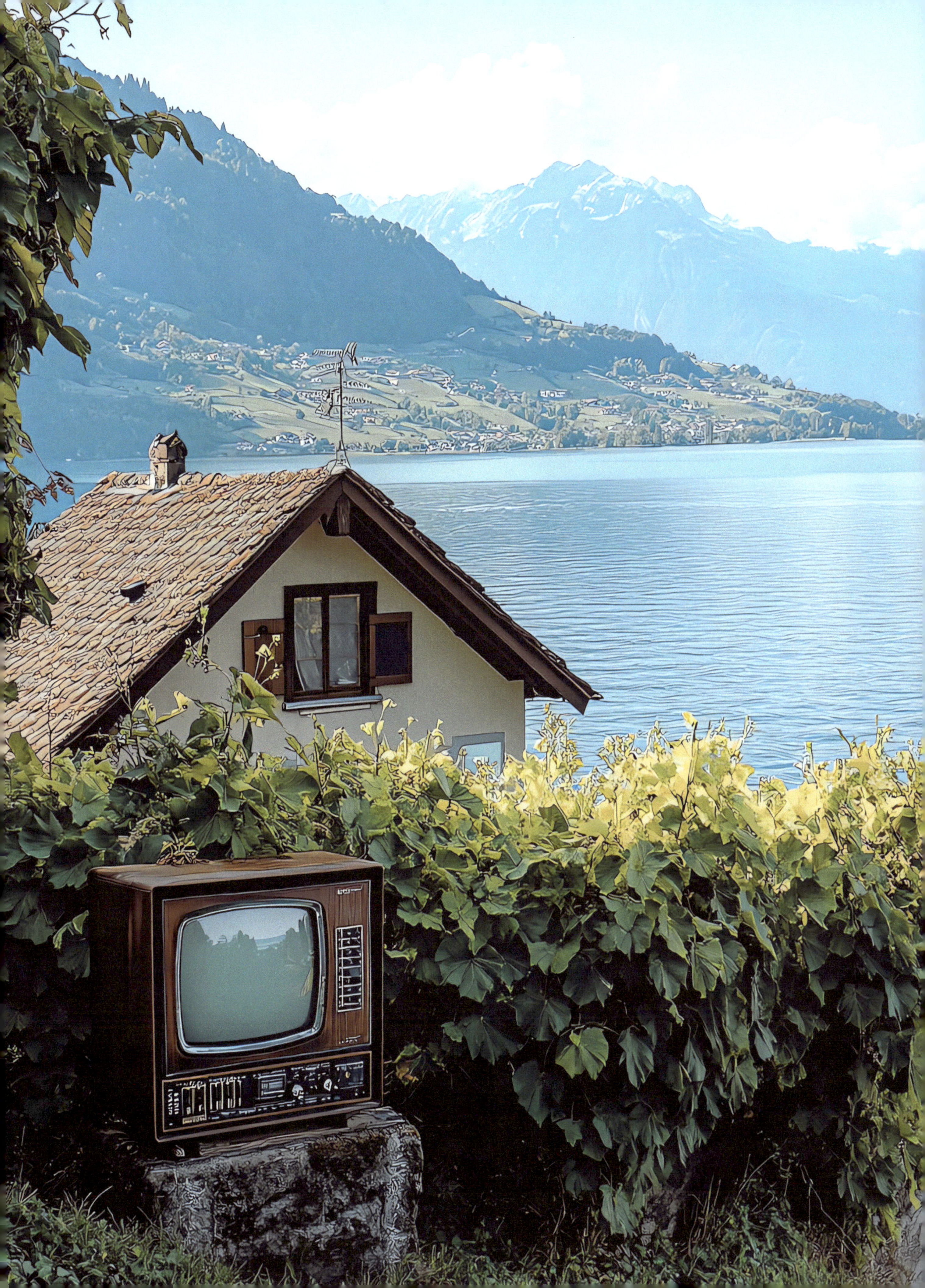

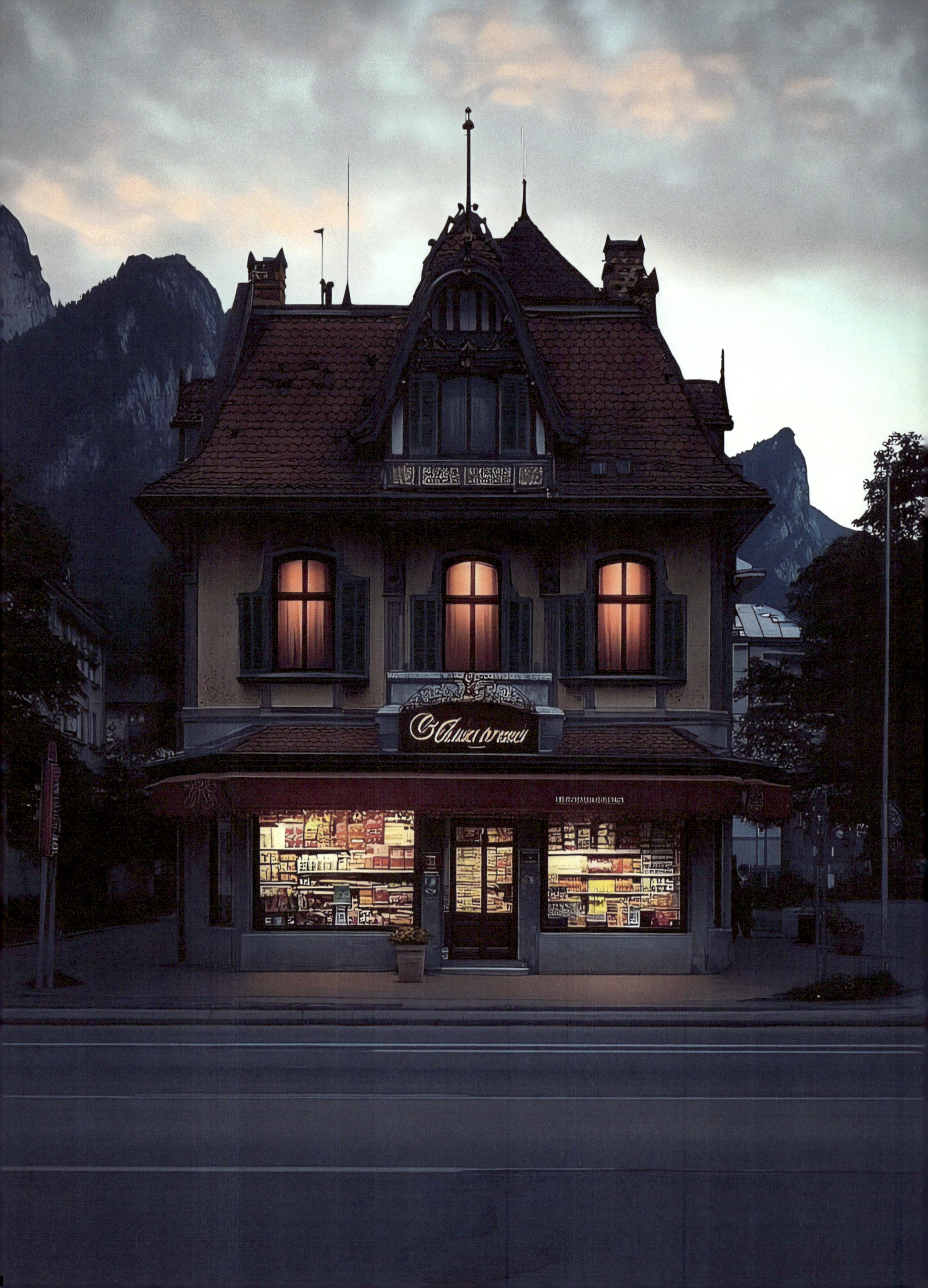

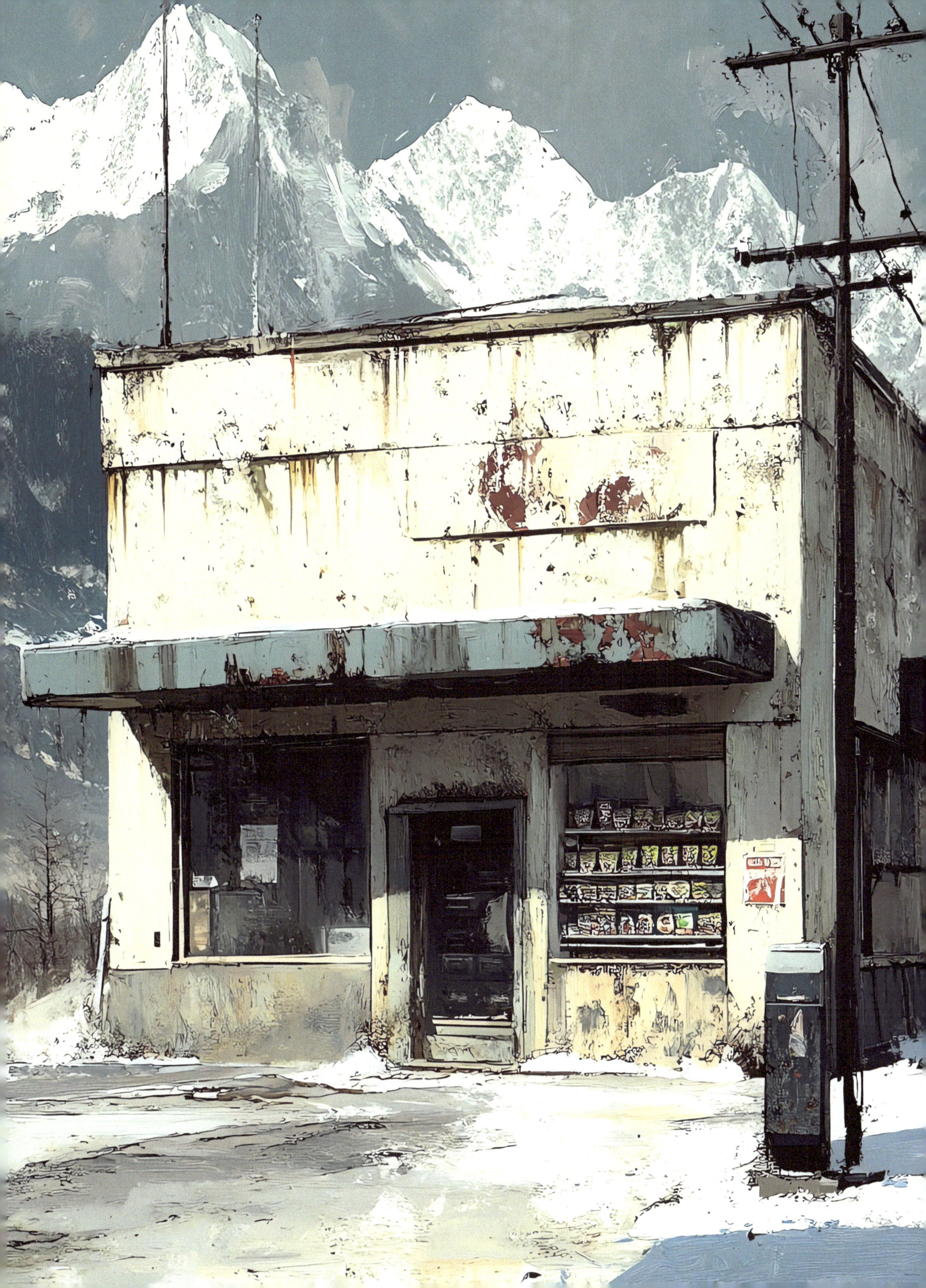

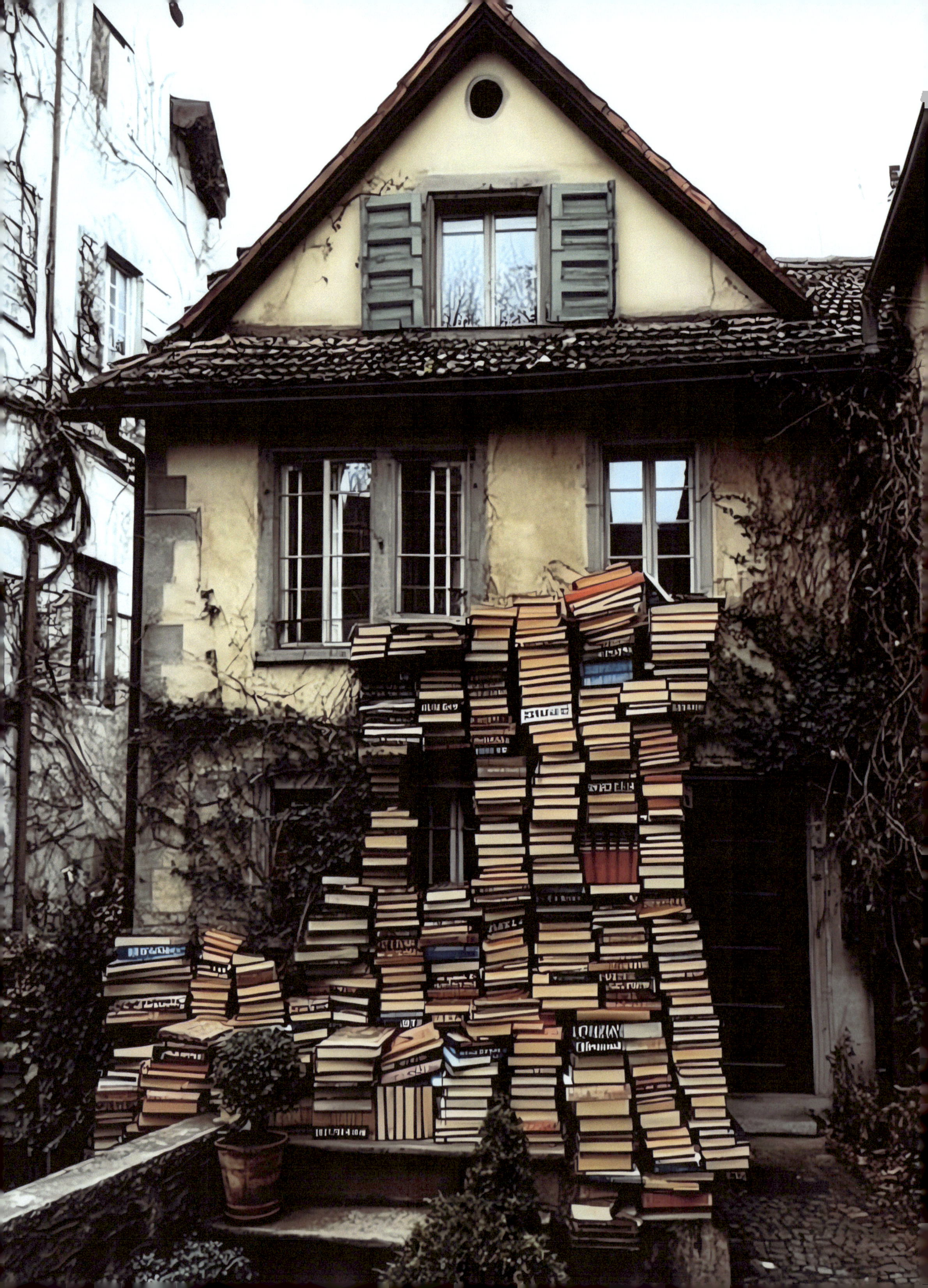

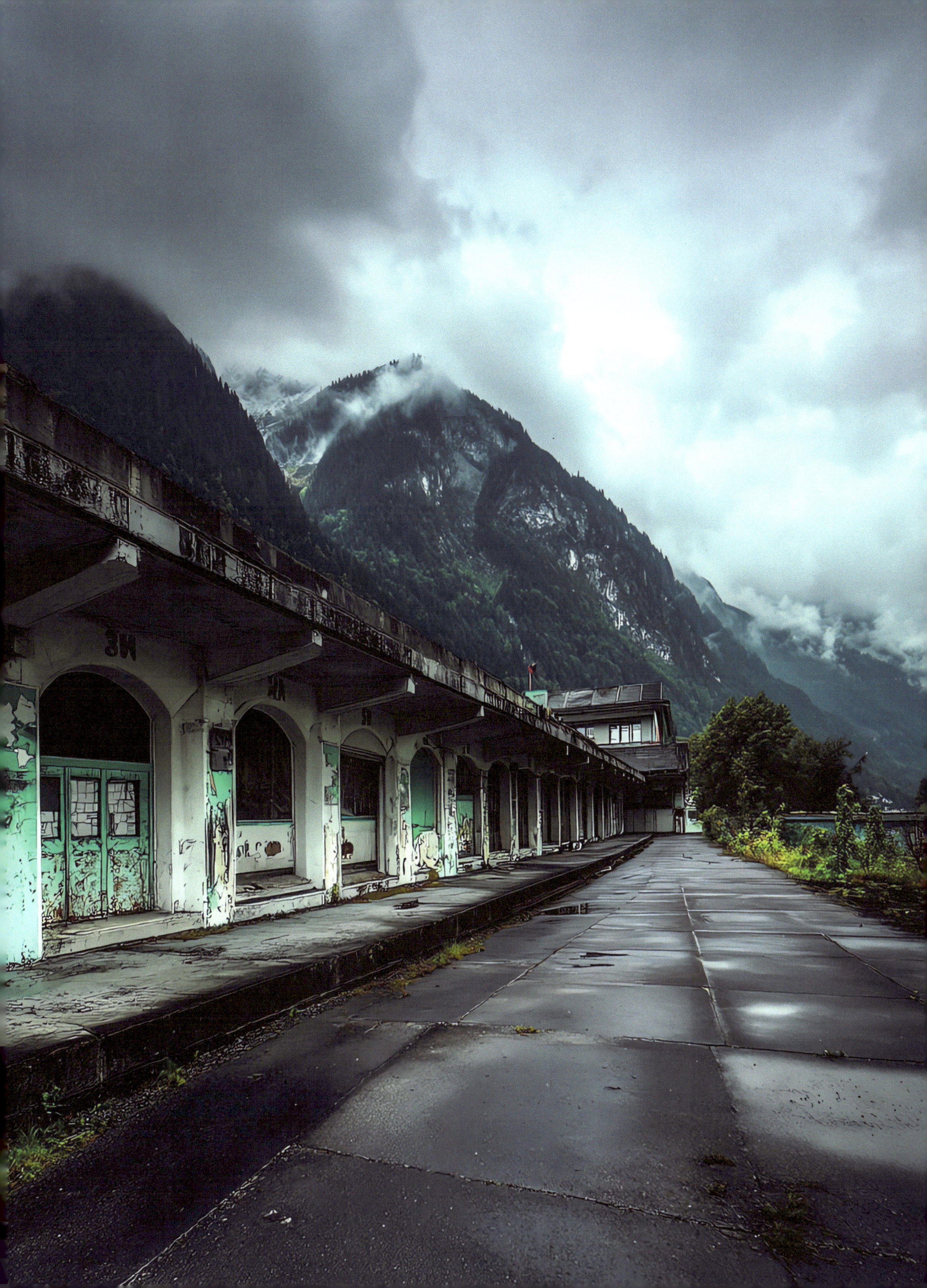

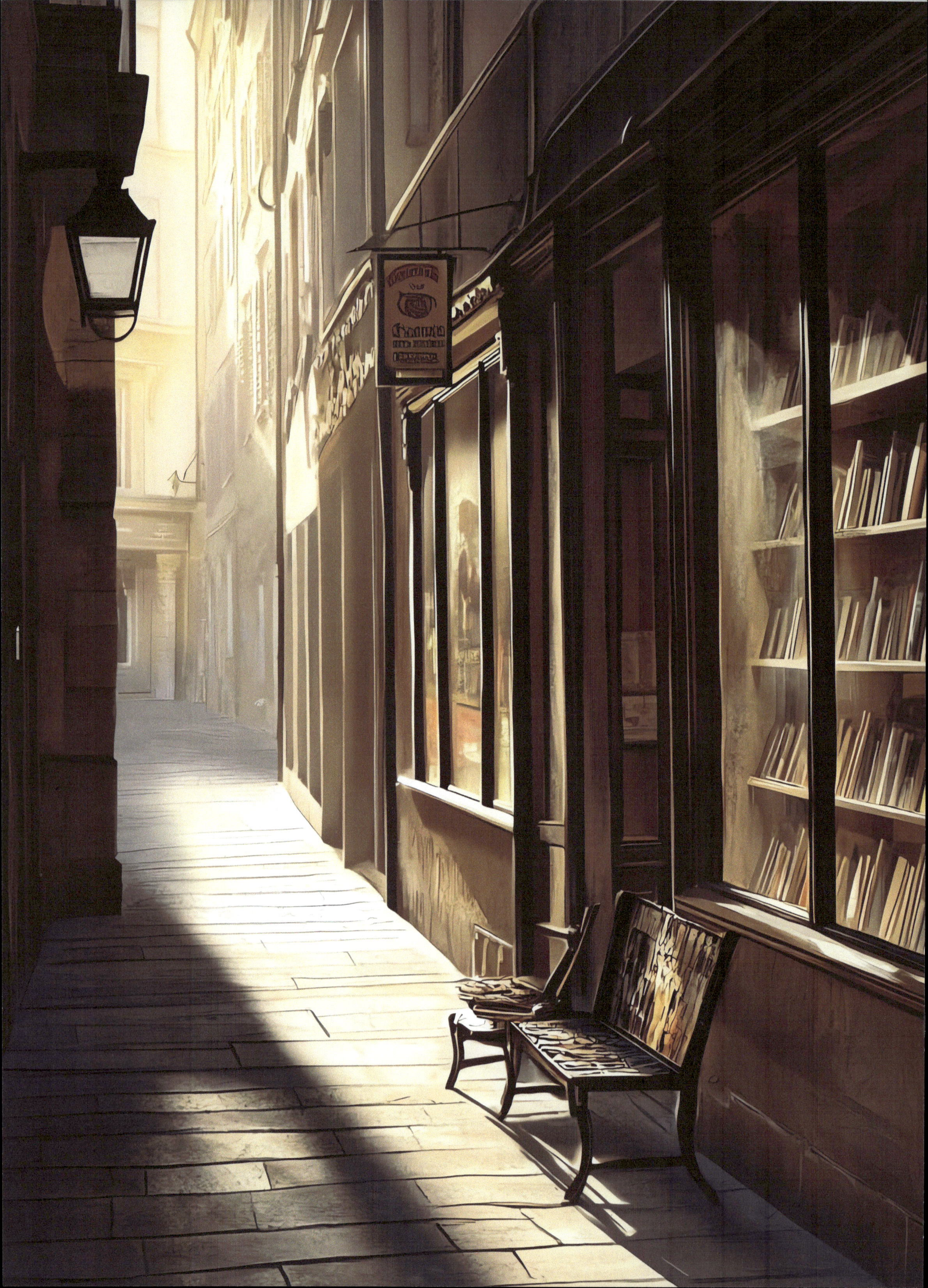

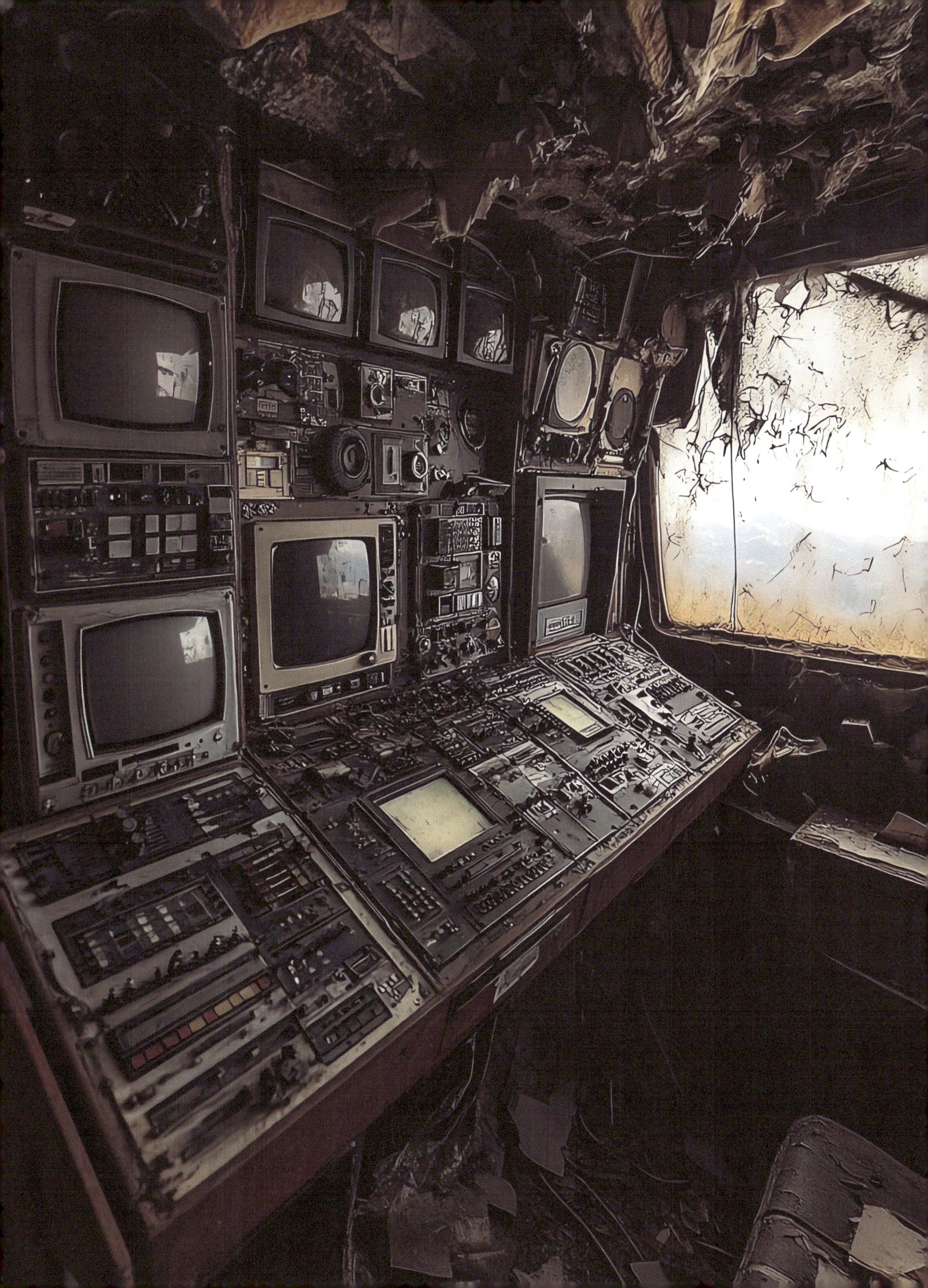

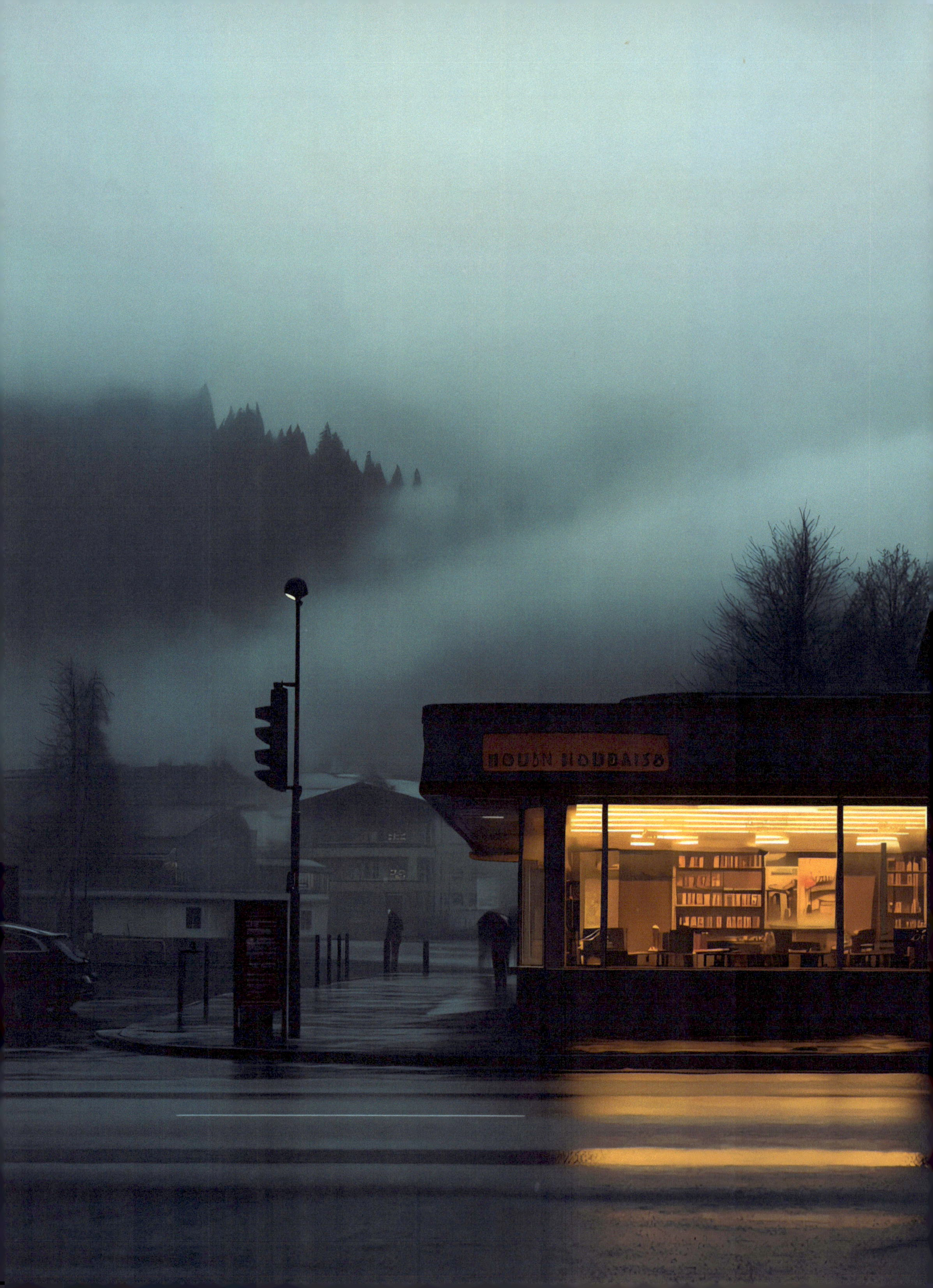

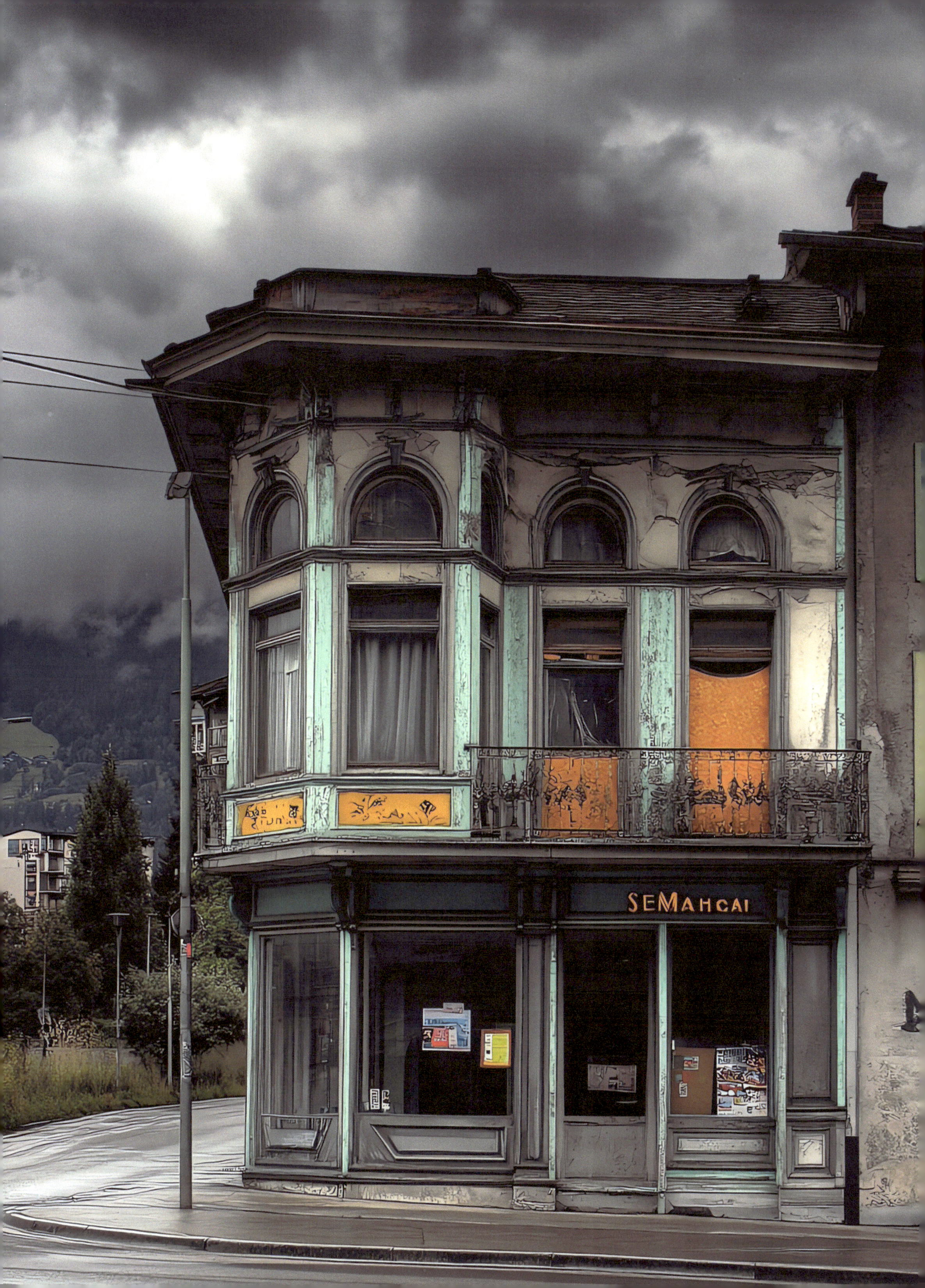
SEMAHCAI

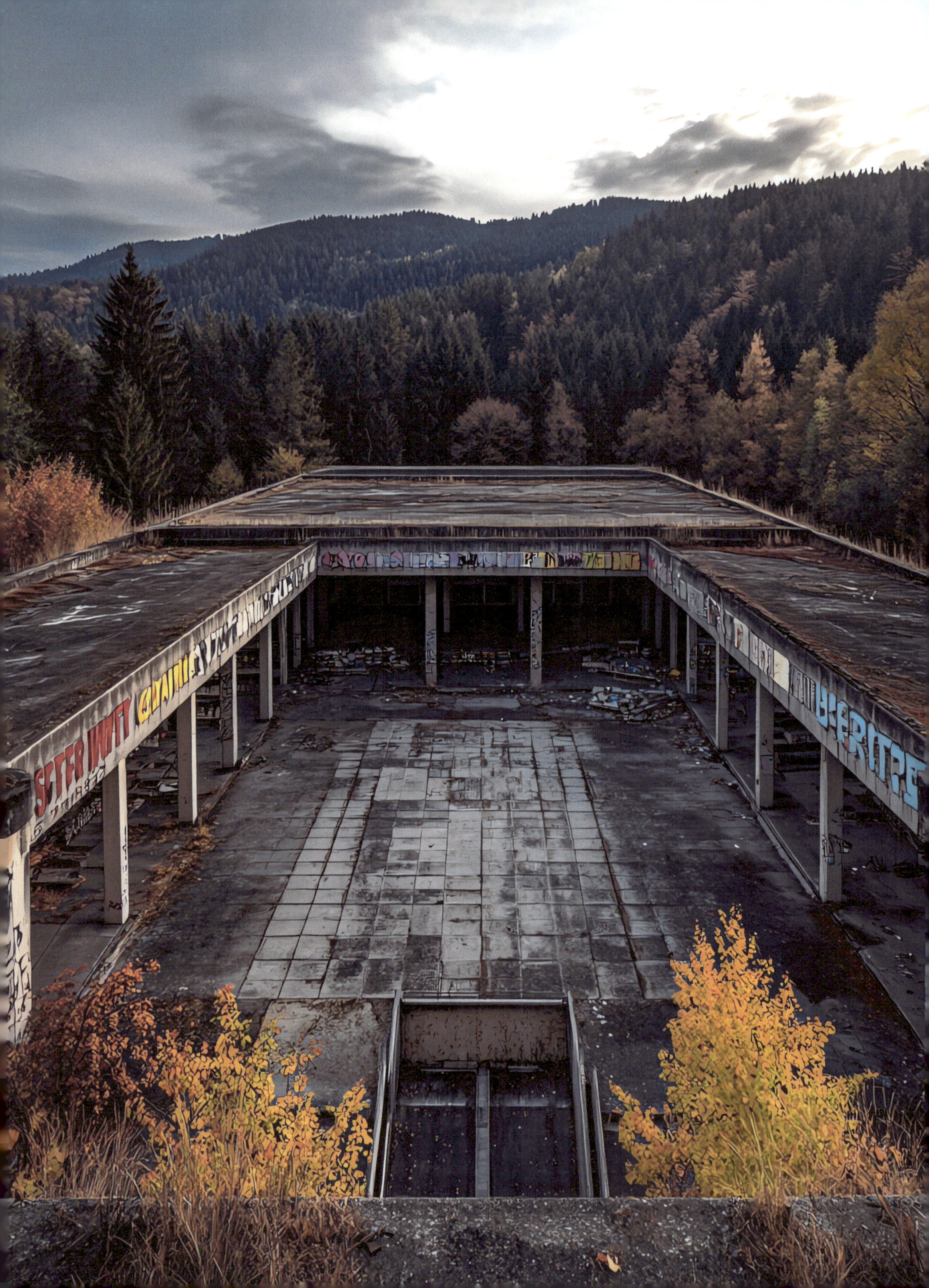

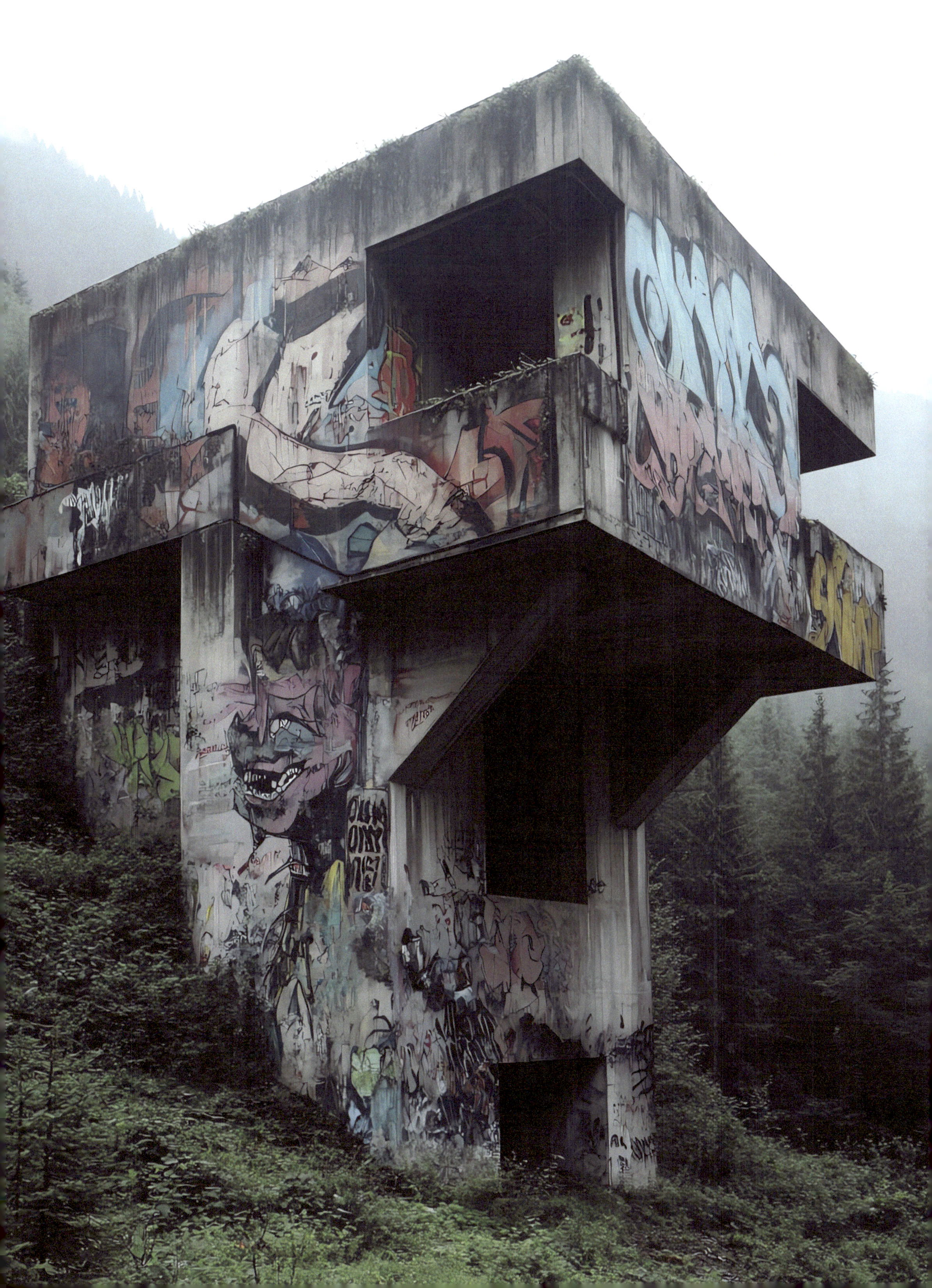

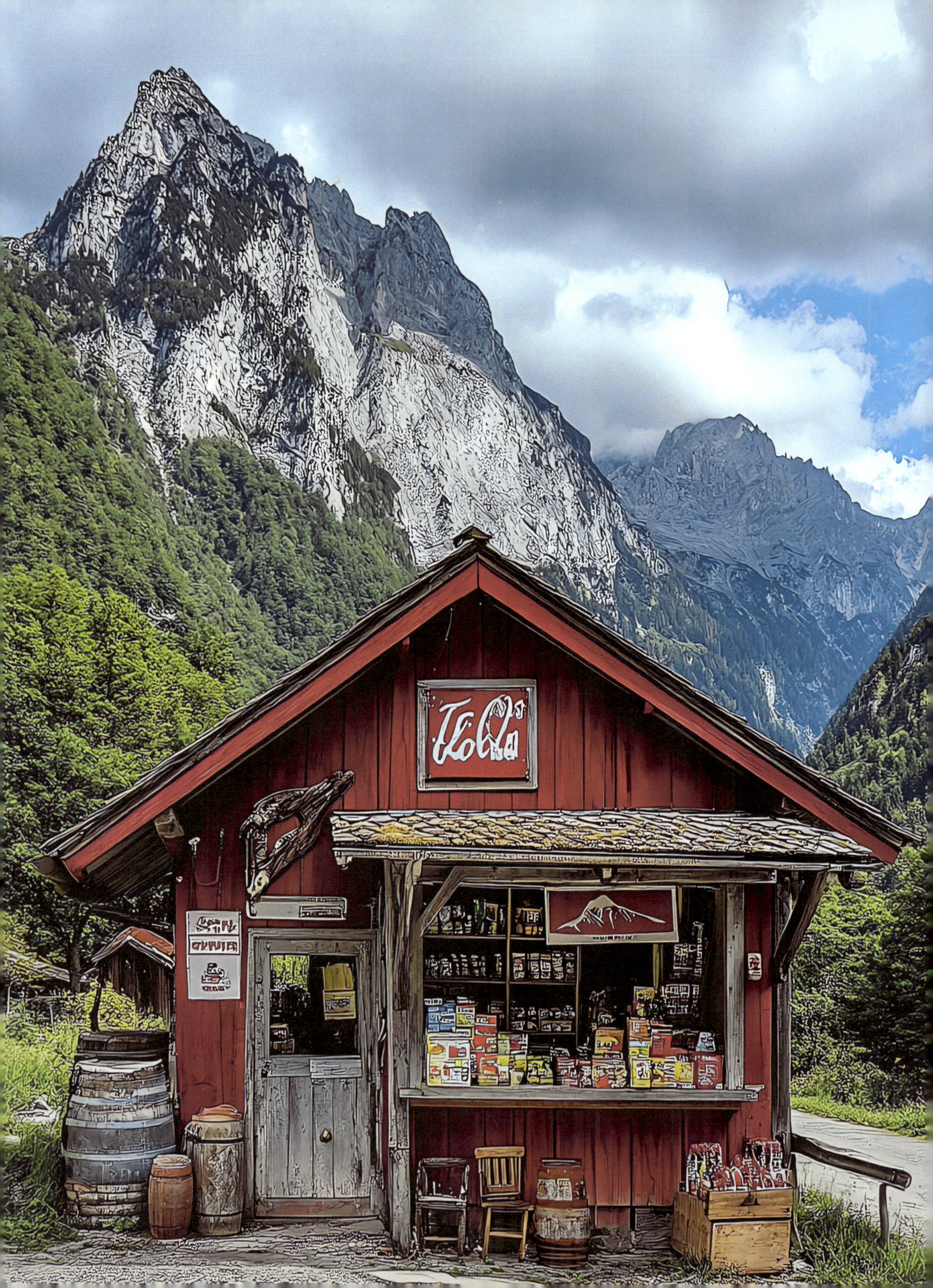

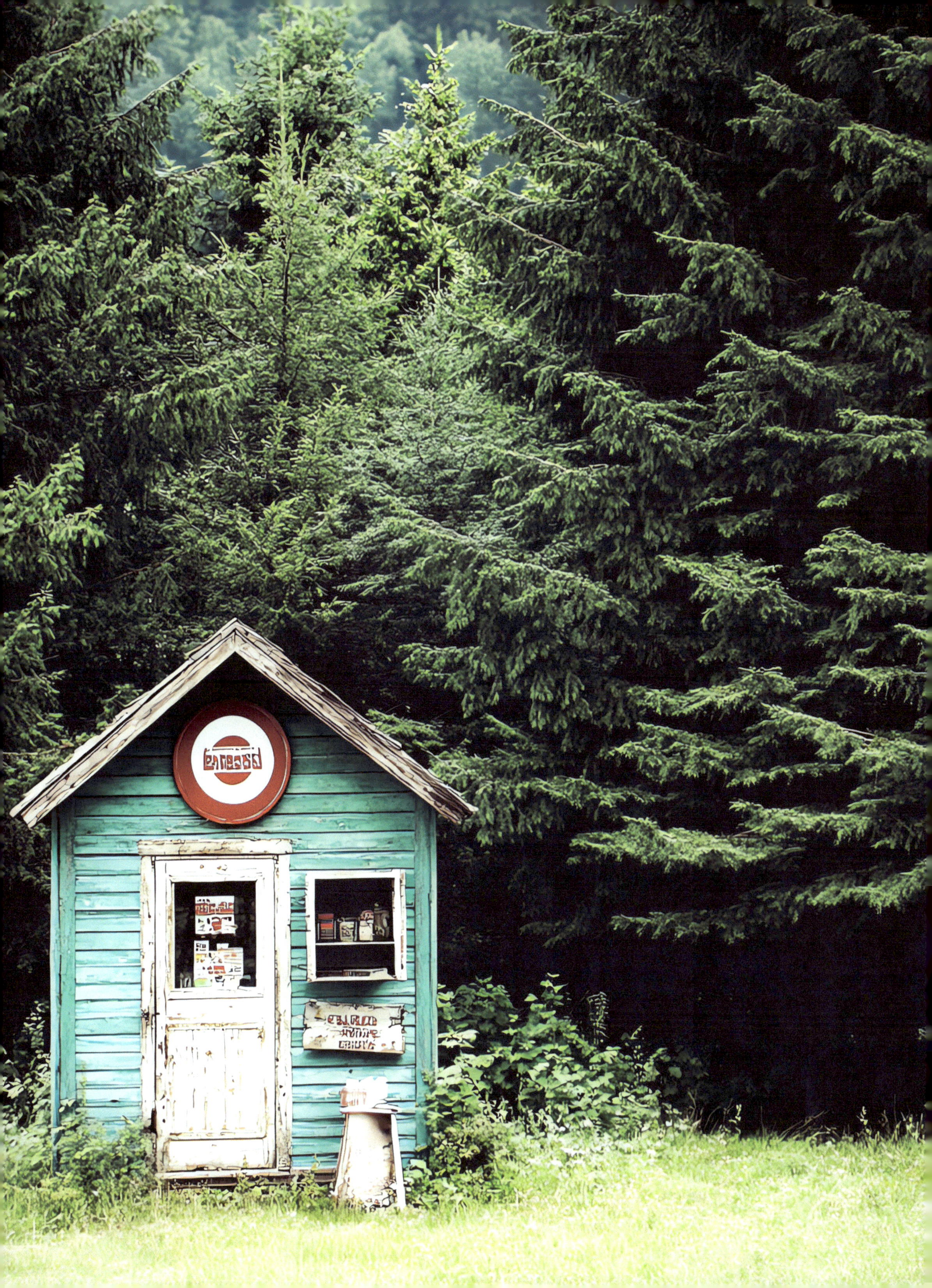

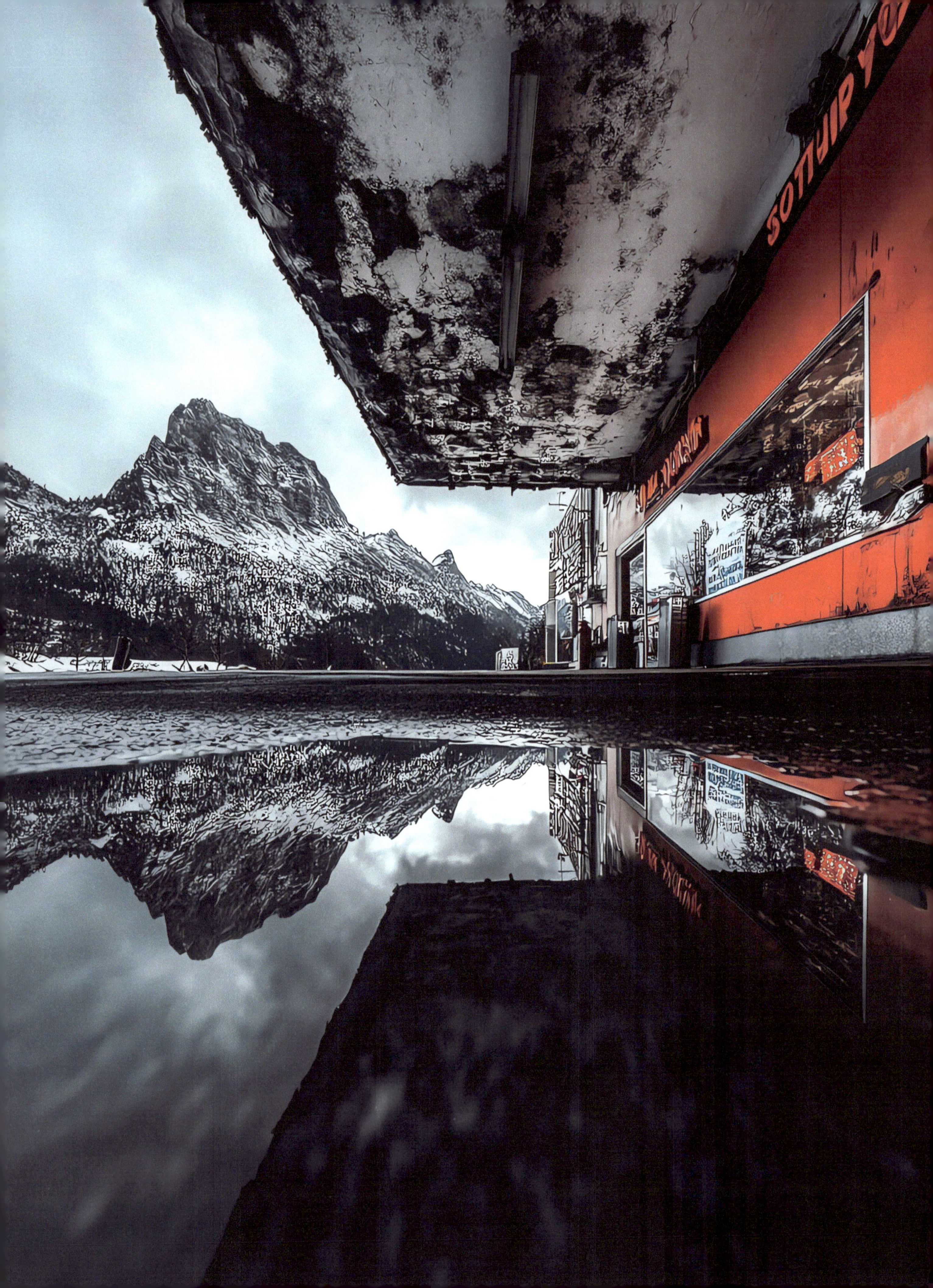

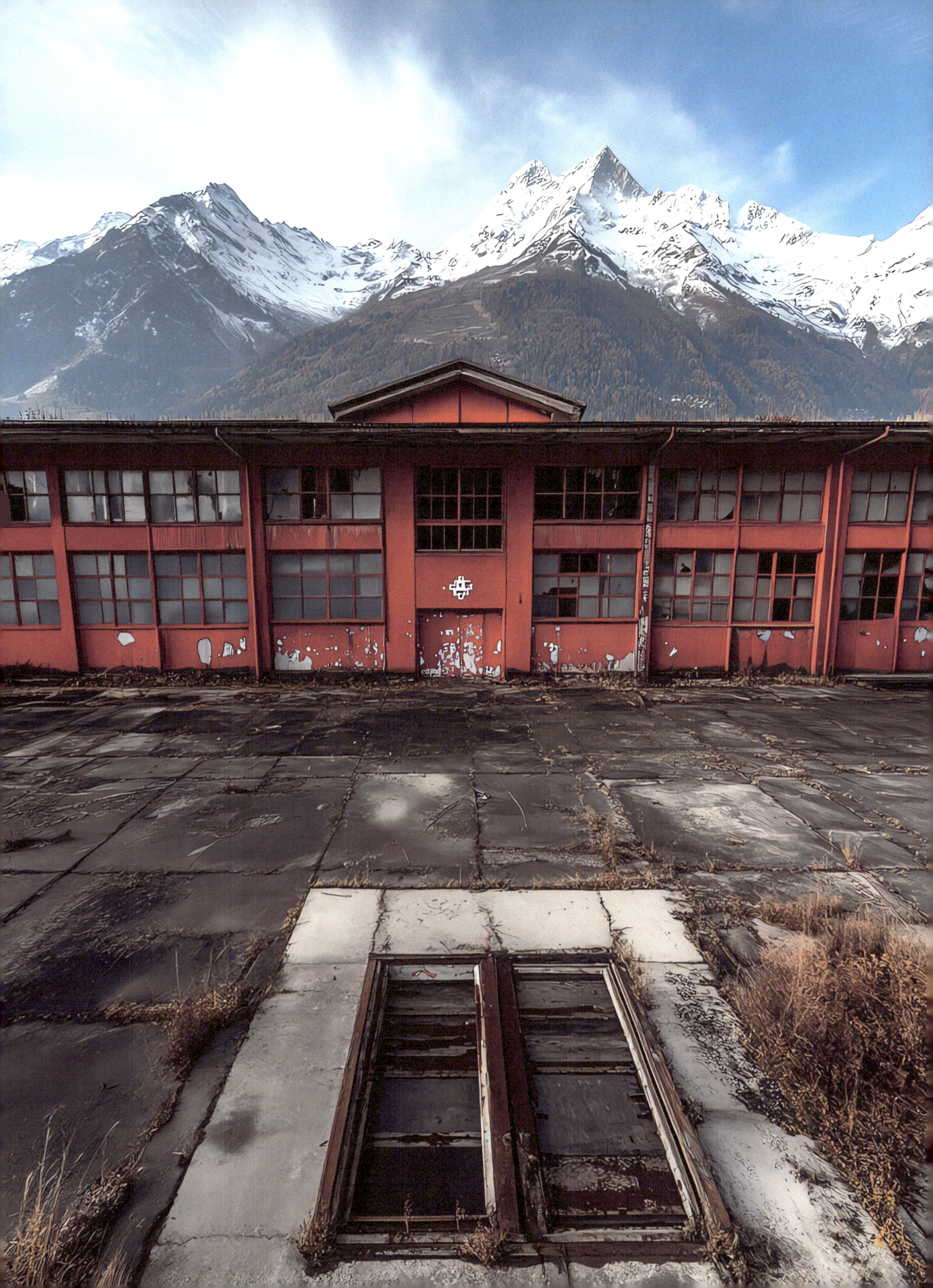

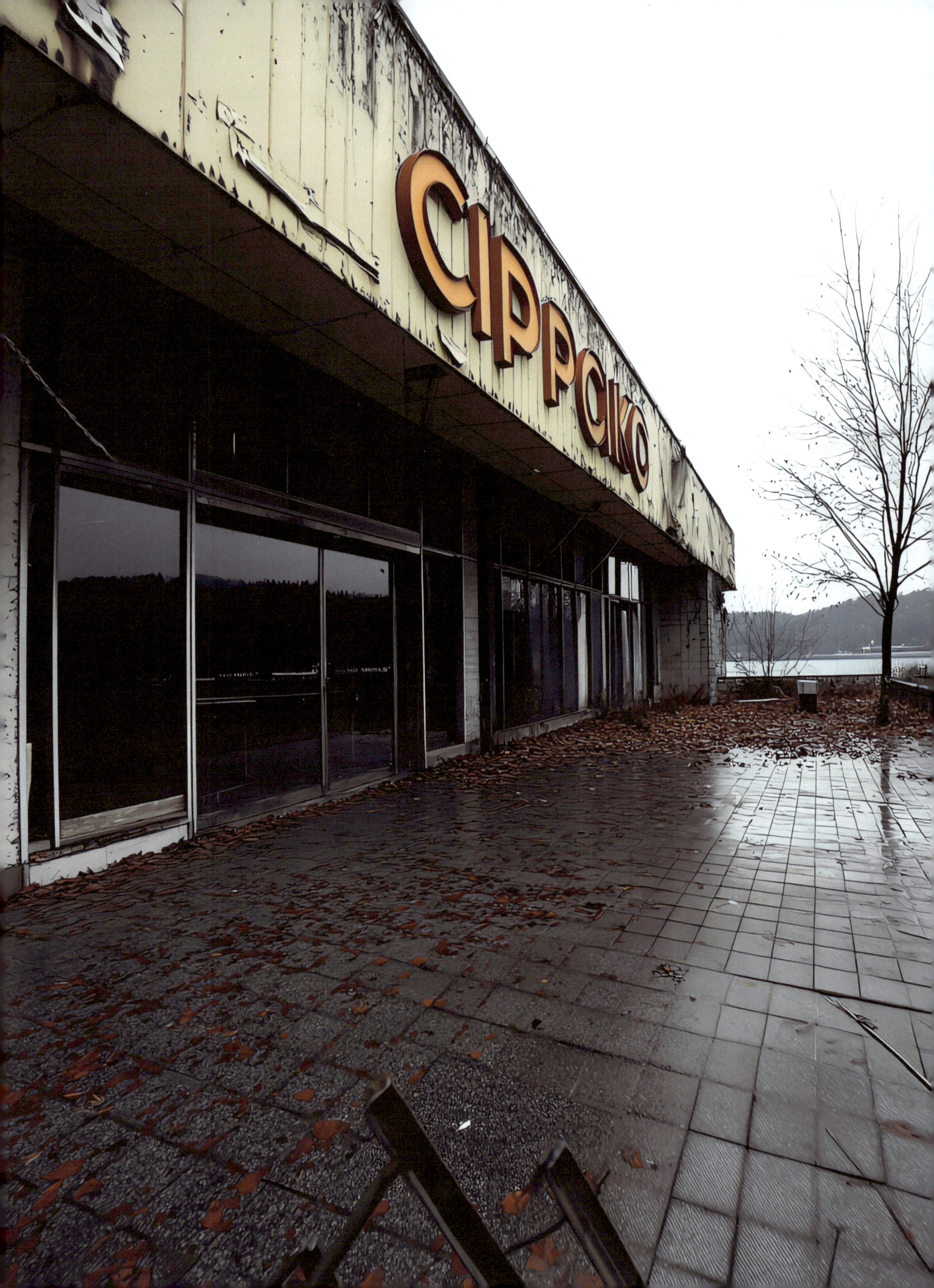

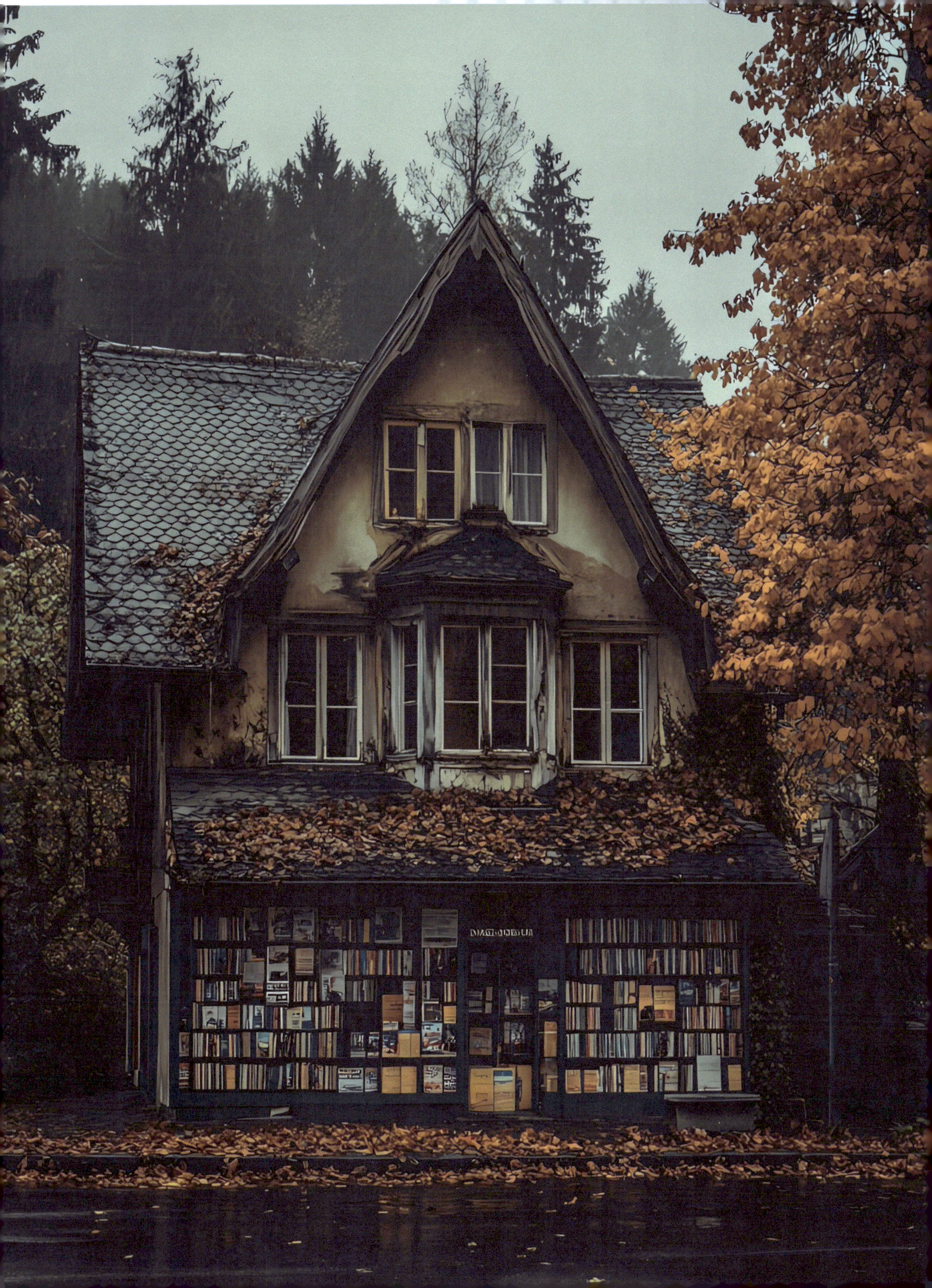

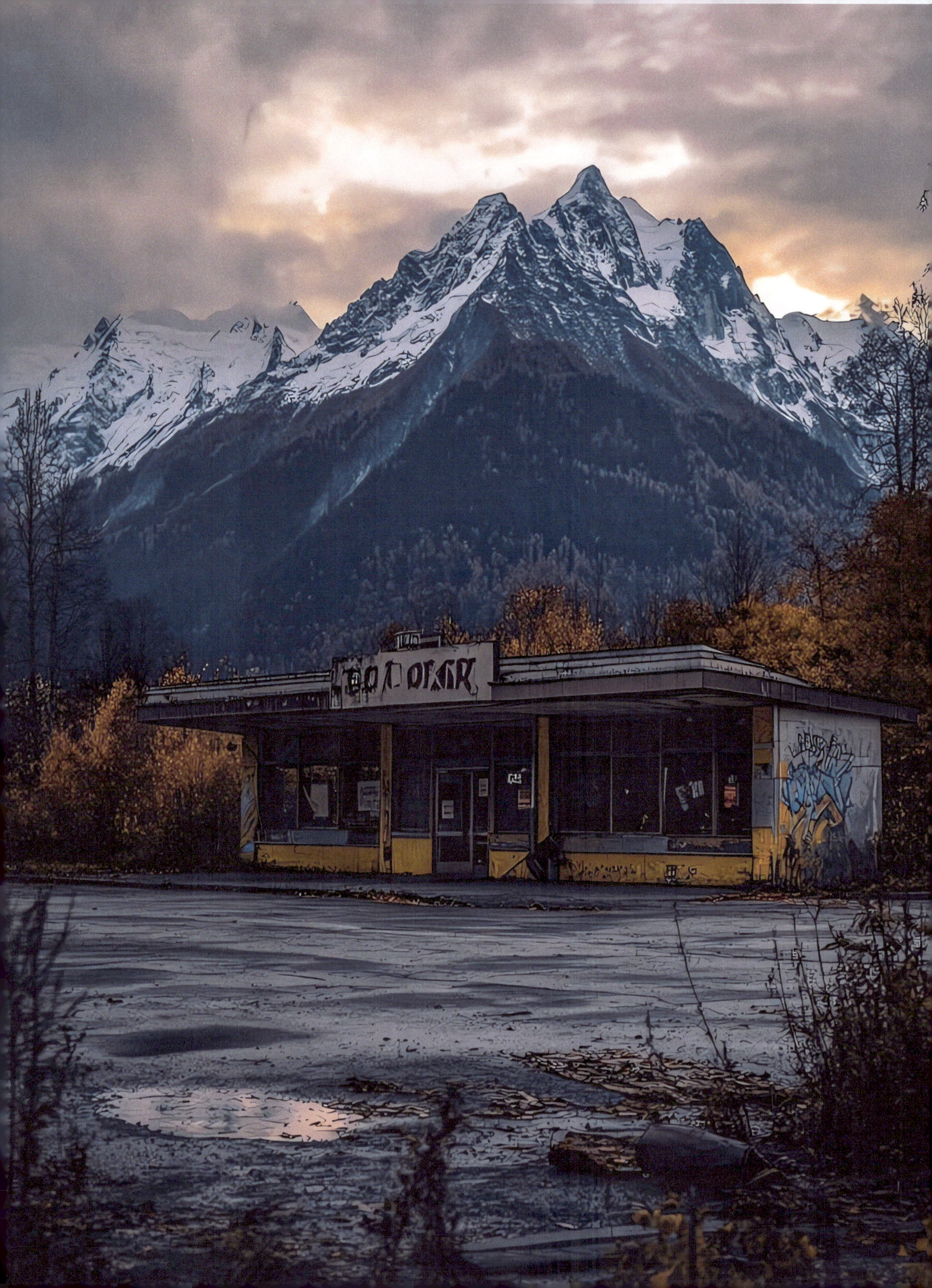

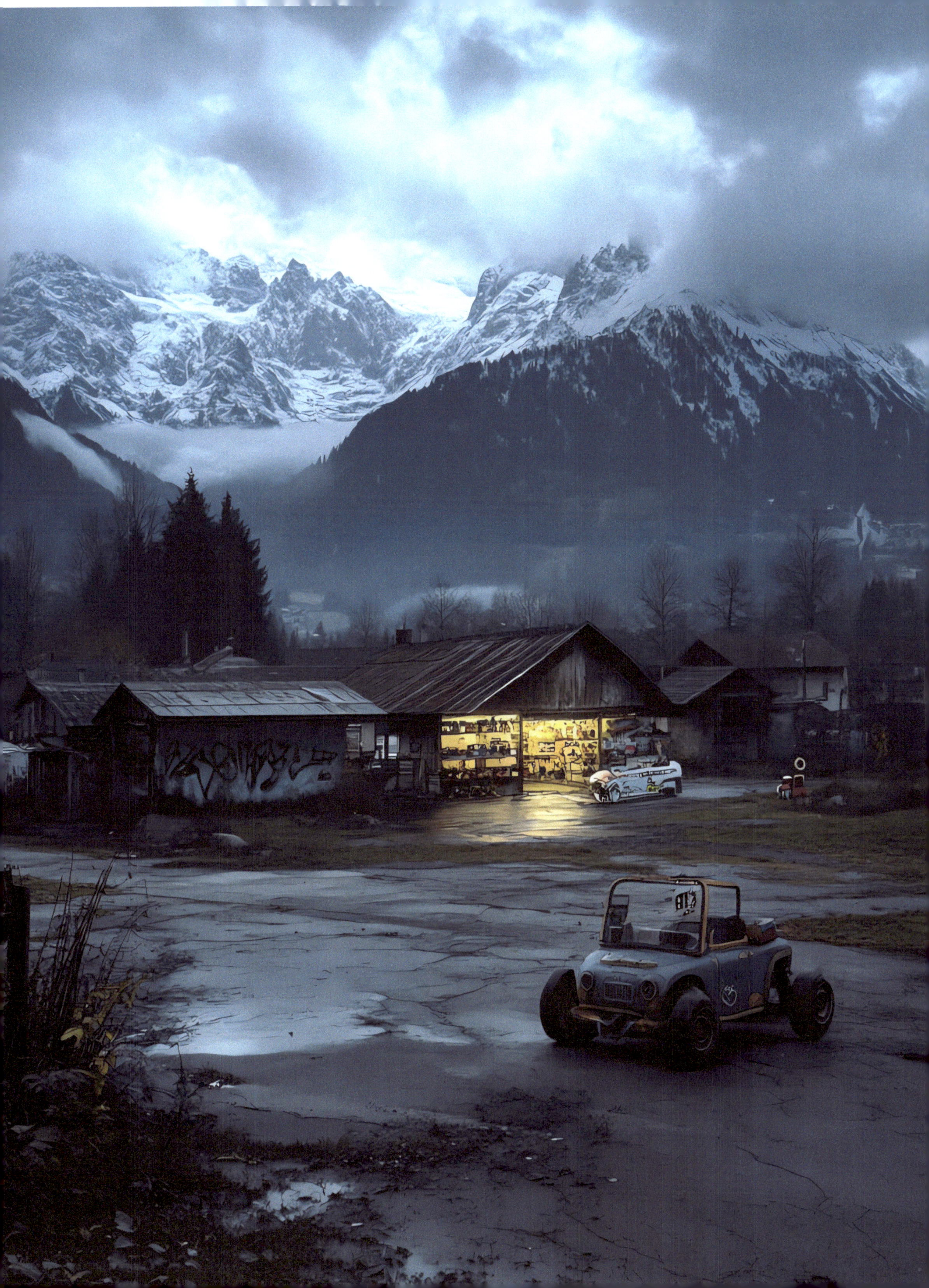

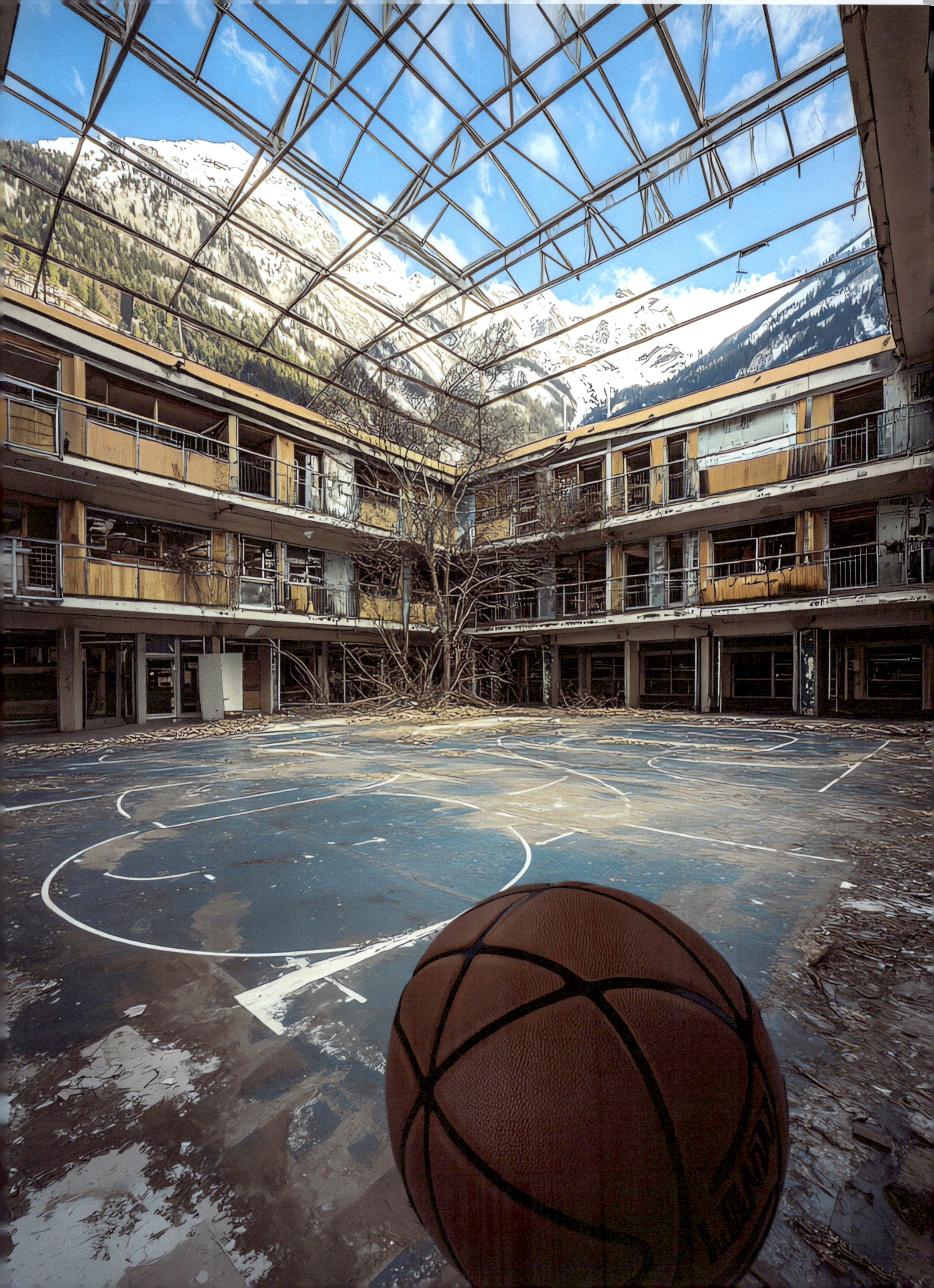

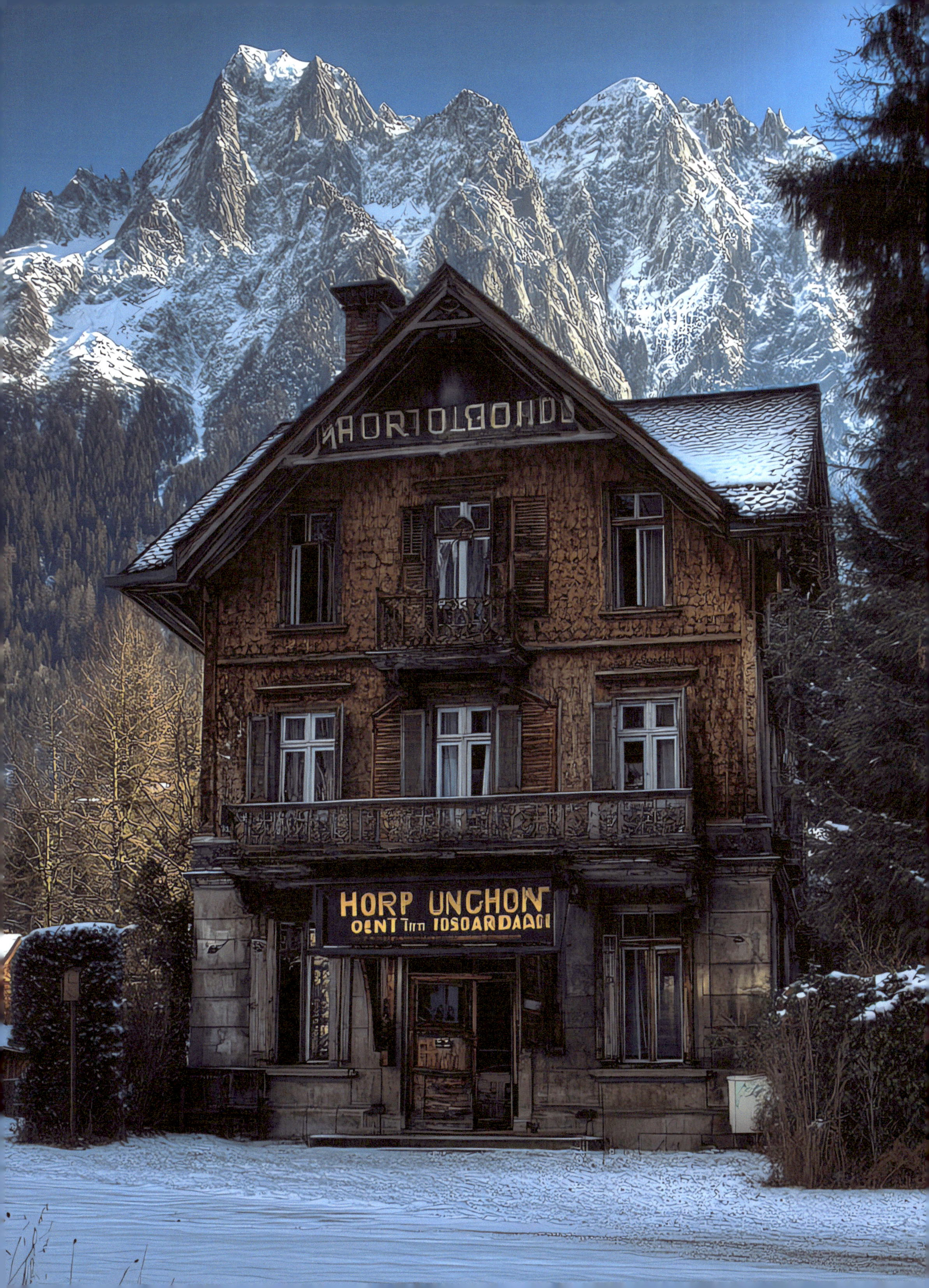
HORP UNCHON

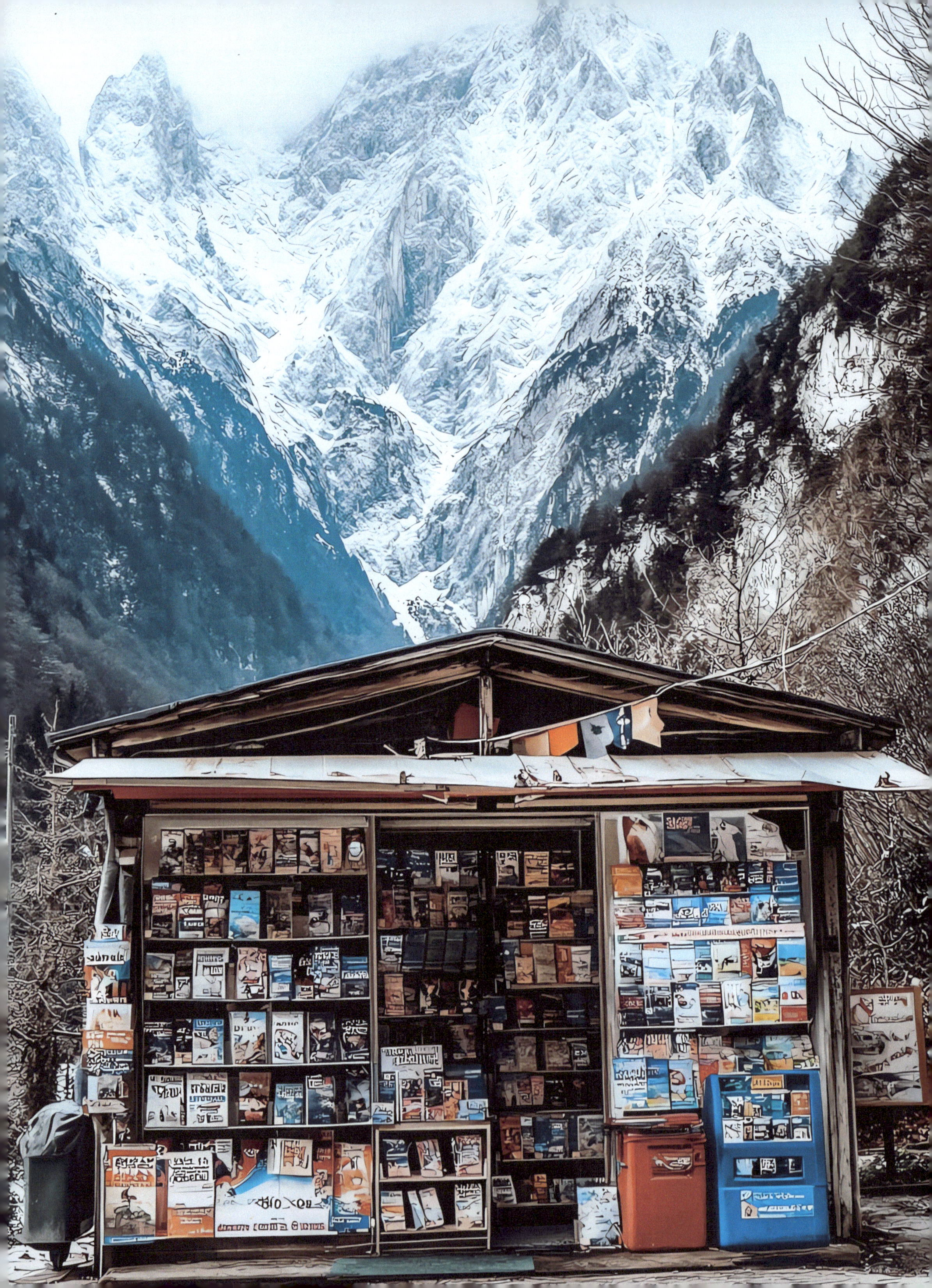

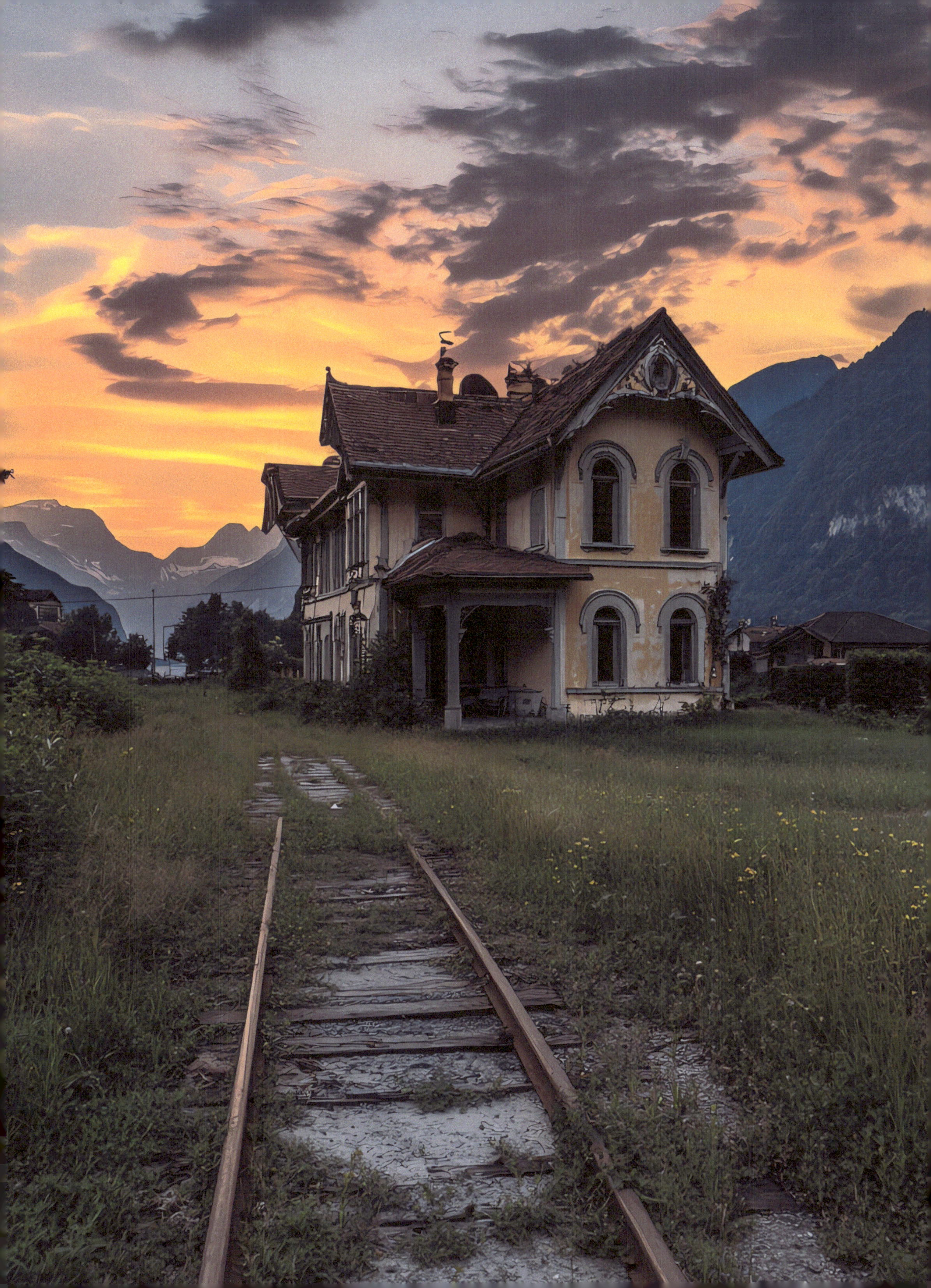

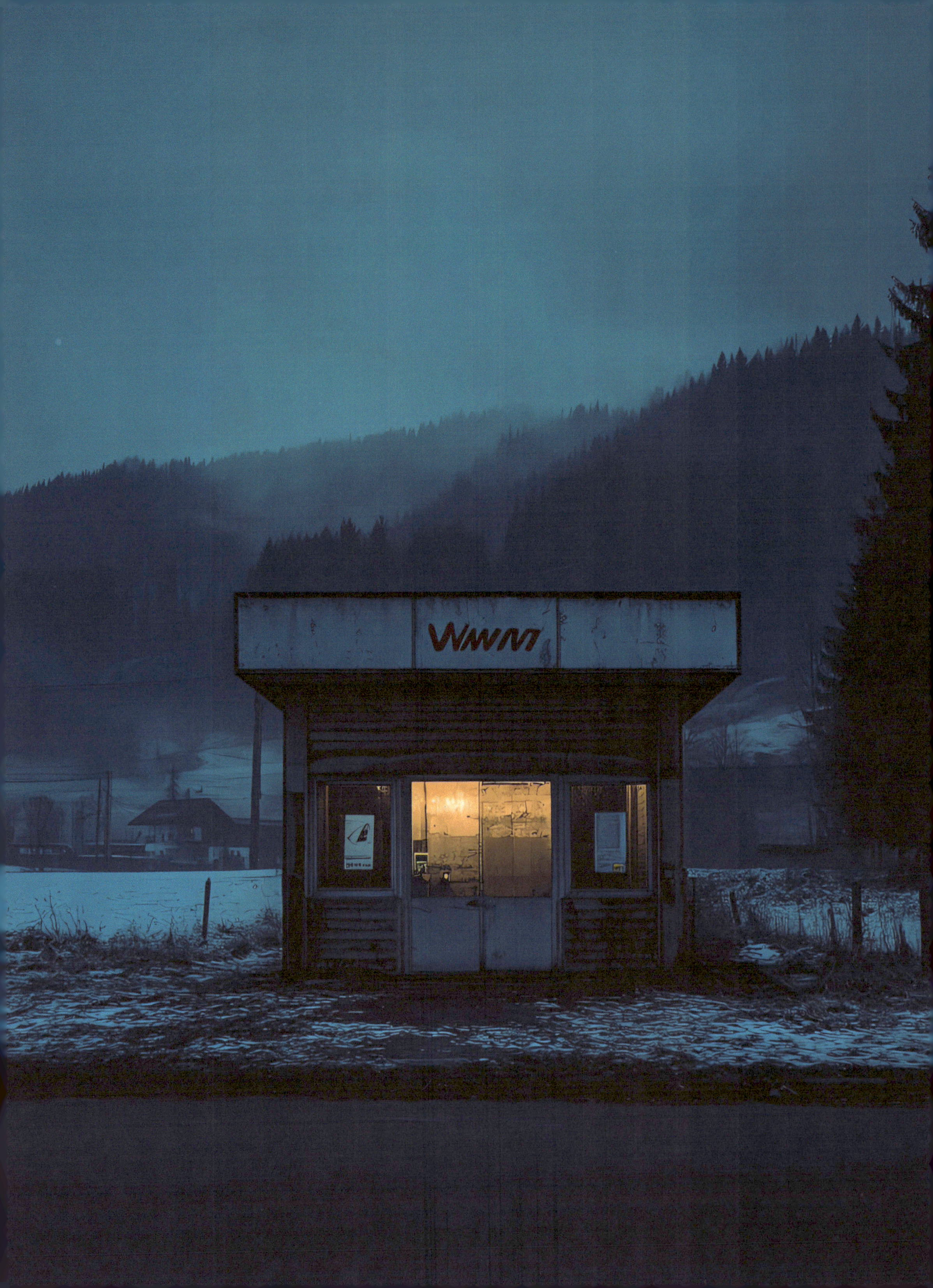

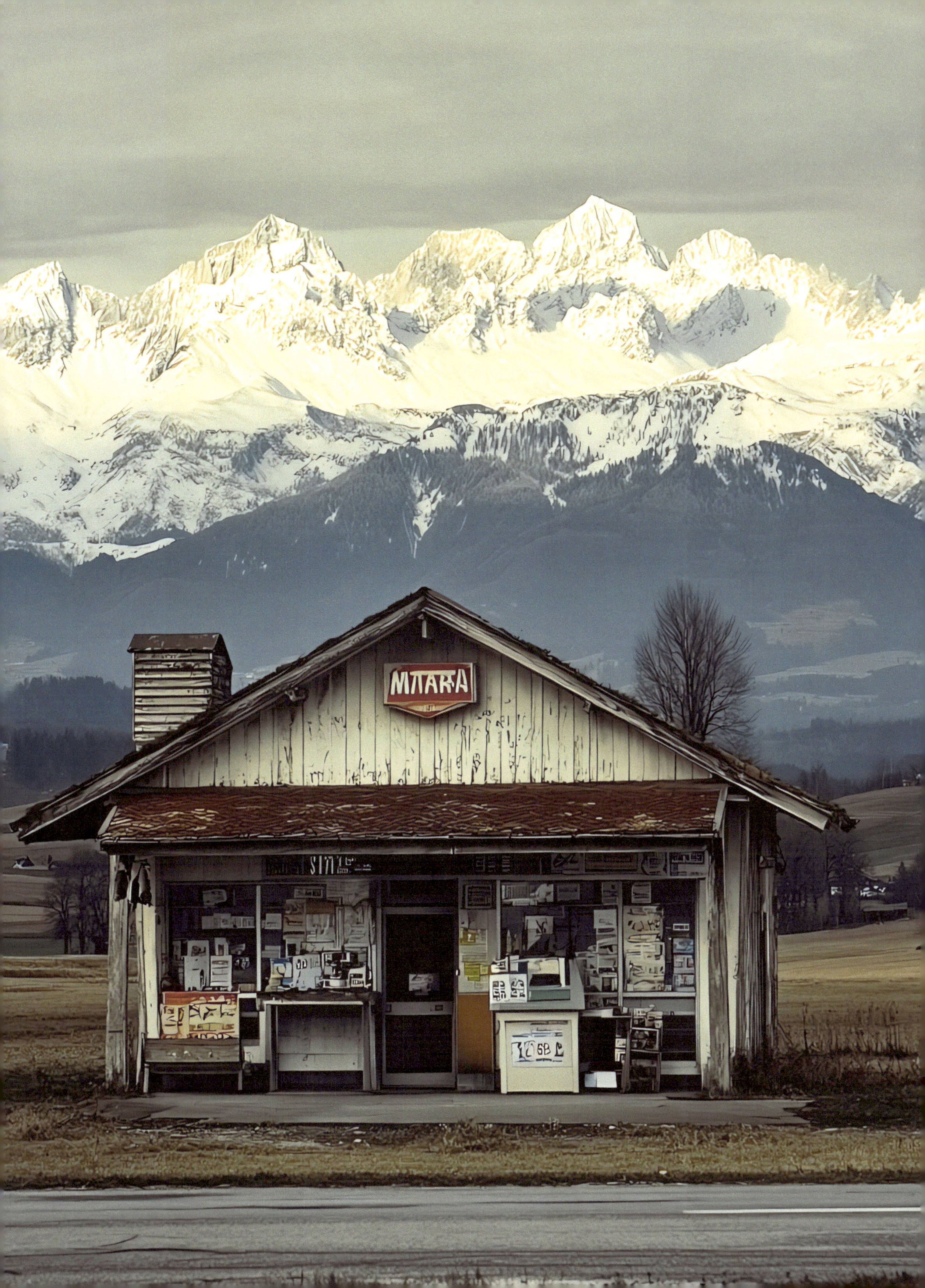

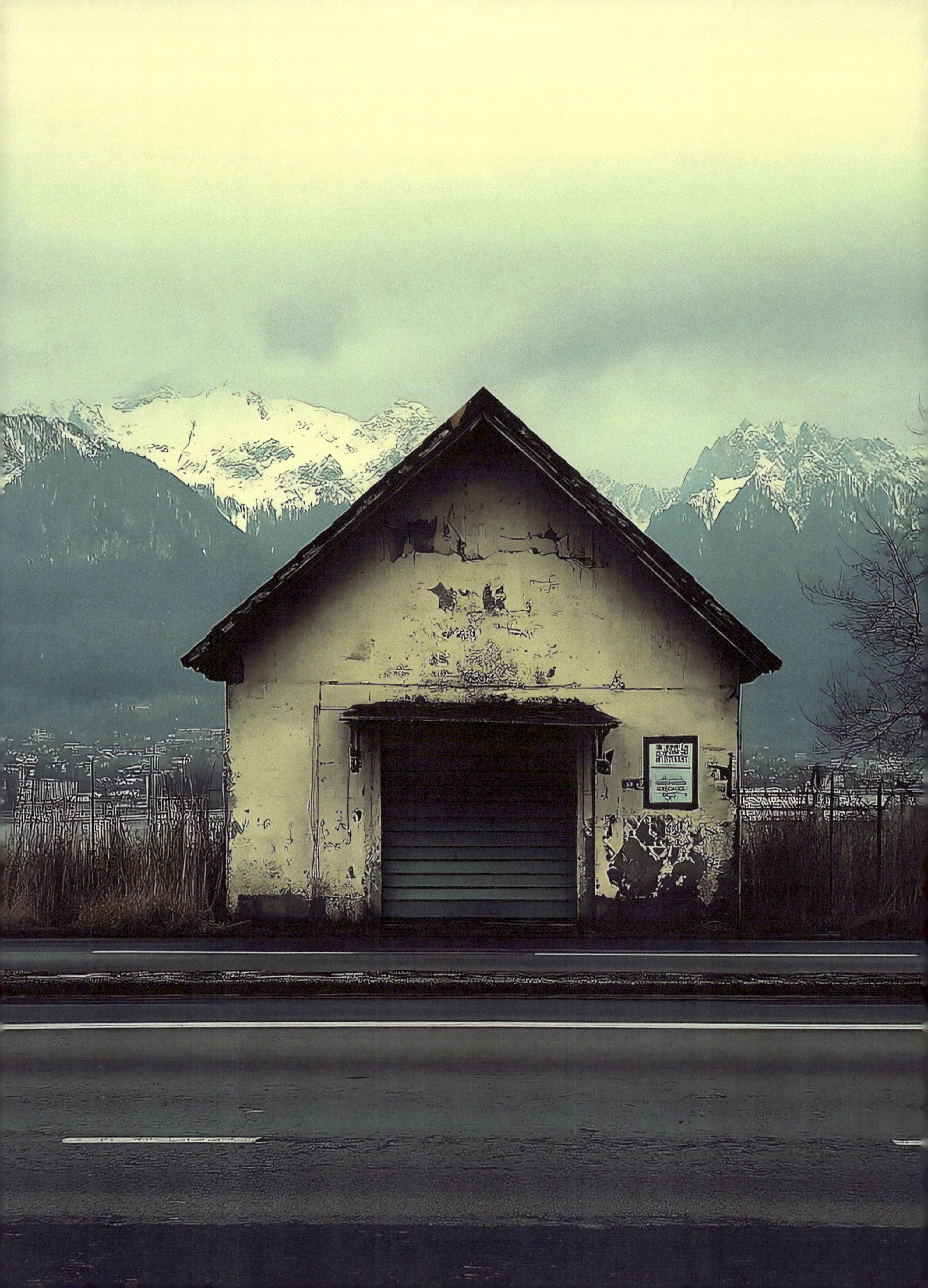

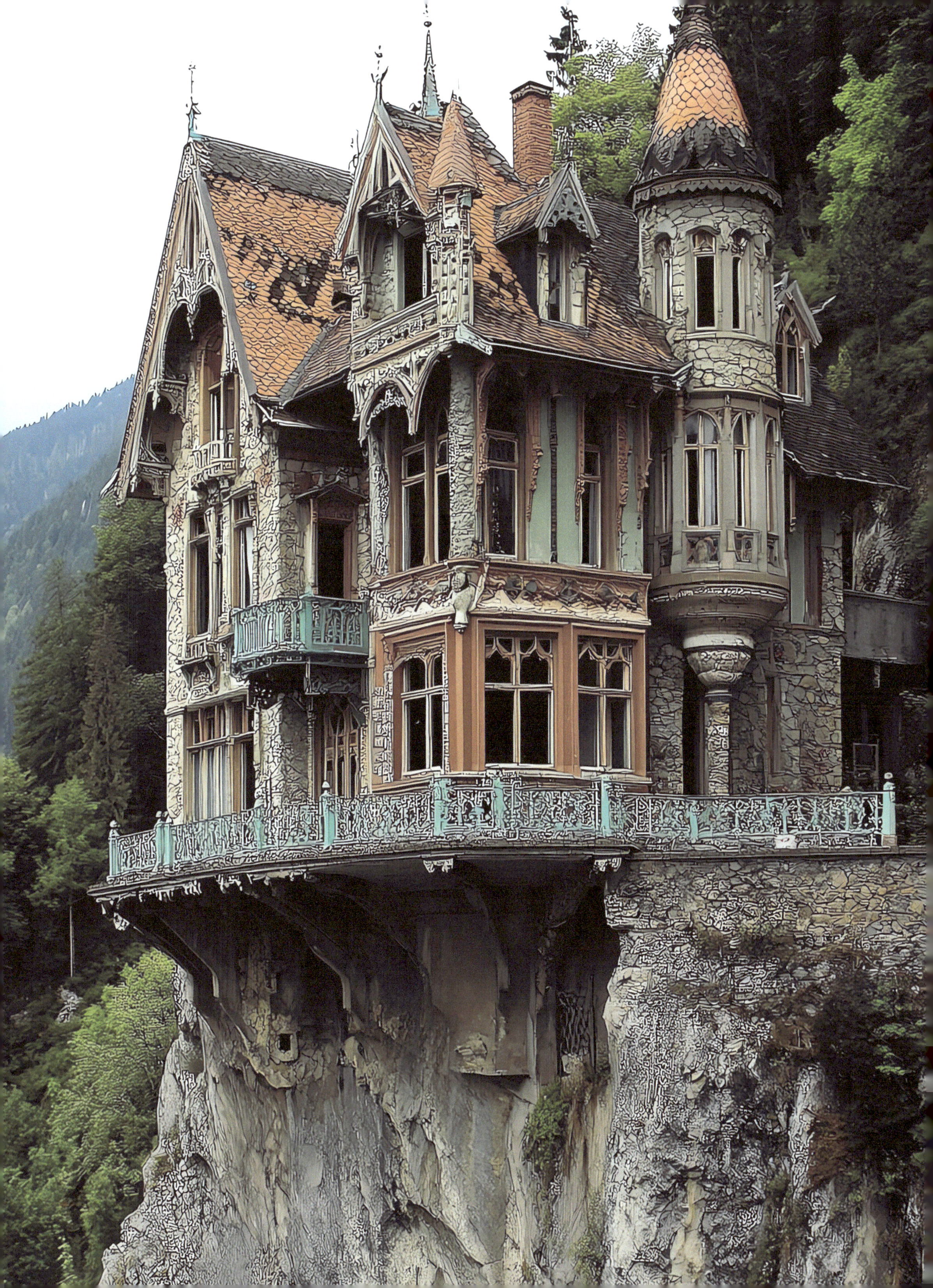

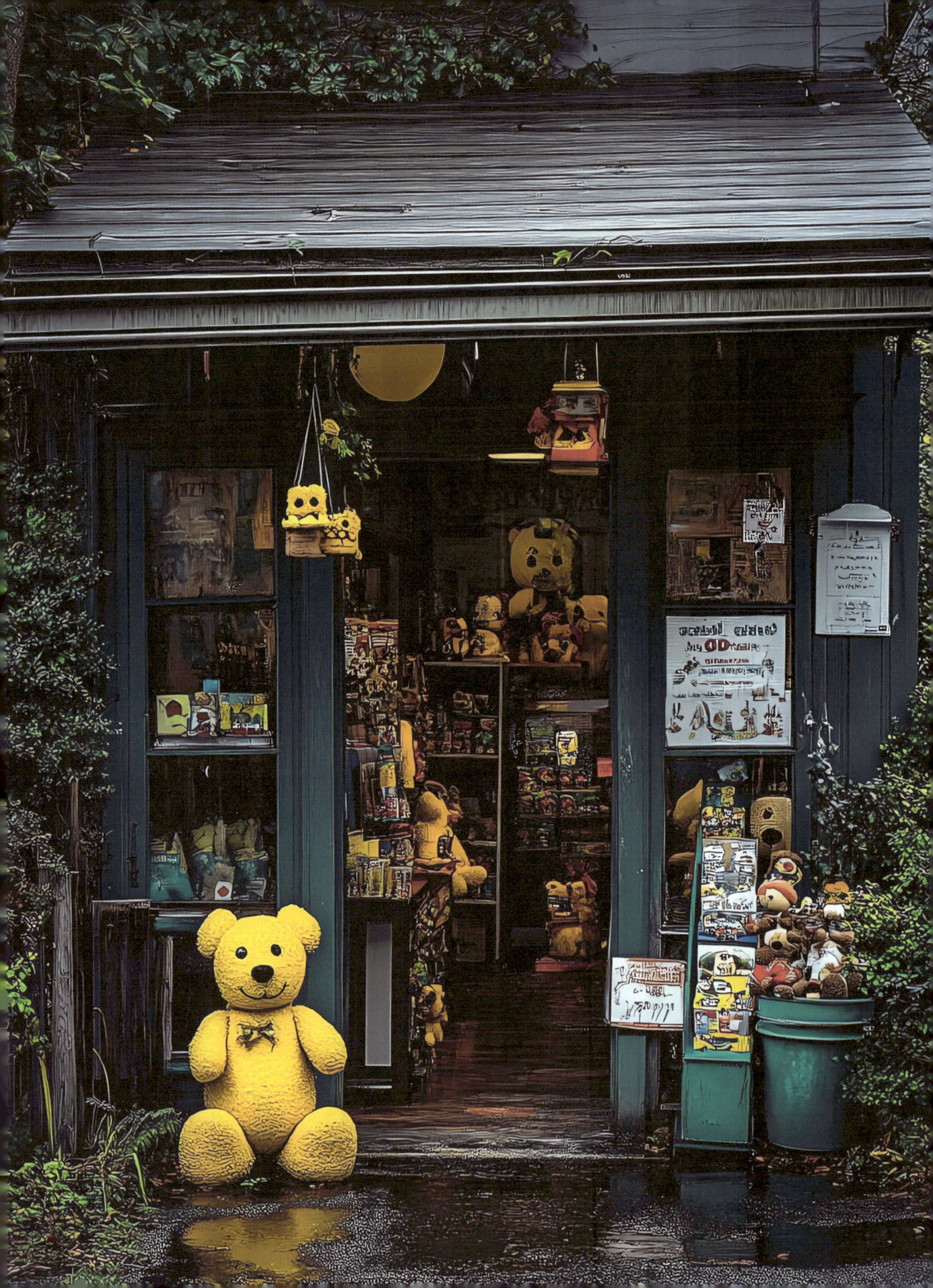

www.ingramcontent.com/pod-product-compliance
Lightning Source LLC
Chambersburg PA
CBHW040420220526
45473CB00004B/1304
* 9 7 9 8 3 0 3 3 4 1 8 4 5 *